Internet Jobs!

The Complete Guide to Finding the Hottest Internet Jobs

John Kador

McGraw-Hill

New York   San Francisco   Washington, D.C.   Auckland   Bogotá Caracas
Lisbon   London   Madrid   Mexico City   Milan
Montreal   New Dehli   San Juan   Singapore
Sydney   Tokyo   Toronto

McGraw-Hill

A Division of The McGraw·Hill Companies

1 2 3 4 5 6 7 8 9 0   AGM/AGM   9 0 9 8 7 6 5 4 3 2 1 0 9

ISBN 0-07-135261-9

The sponsoring editor for this book was Betsy N. Brown, the editing supervisor was John M. Morriss, and the production supervisor was Tina Cameron. It was set in Palatino by BookMasters, Inc.

Printed and bound by Quebecor Printing.

This publication is designed to provide accurate and authoritative information in regard to the subject matter covered. It is sold with the understanding that the publisher is not engaged in rendering legal, accounting, or other professional service. If legal advice or other expert assistance is required, the services of a competent professional person should be sought.

 This book is printed on recycled, acid-free paper containing a minimum of 50 percent recycled de-inked fiber.

McGraw-Hill books are available at special quantity discounts to use as premiums and sales promotions, or for use in corporate training programs. For more information, please write to the Director of Special Sales, McGraw-Hill, 11 West 19th Street, New York, NY 10011. Or contact your local bookstore.

To Anna Beth

Wealth in the new regime flows directly from innovation, not optimization;
that is, wealth is not gained by perfecting the known,
but by imperfectly seizing the unknown.

—Kevin Kelly
New Rules for the New Economy, *Wired*

Contents

Why Read This Book?

You have in your hands a resource that can help you navigate the dizzying world of Net jobs. *Internet Jobs!* will help you:

- Understand the new rules of the Net Economy.
- Determine the specific skill sets, technical and otherwise, that are most in demand.
- Discern the Internet careers roles that are available right now, those that are emerging, and those that are on the wane.
- Demonstrate that you have the skill sets employers need.

Internet Jobs! addresses these questions:

- What's a Net job?
- How is a Net job different from a traditional job?
- What exactly makes a Net job different?
- What skills are expected of me to get a Net job?
- What new ways of thinking lead to Net jobs?
- What do Net jobs pay?
- What are some of the hottest Net companies?
- Where are some of the best places to live for Net jobs?
- Are Net jobs for me?

If these are your questions . . .

- How do I use the Internet to search for an Internet job?
- How should I prepare my resume for e-posting?
- Should I post my resume on Internet search engines?
- Where are the best job sites for my field?
- Are there special interviewing or negotiating skills I should know about?

. . . keep looking.

Internet Jobs! is not a how-to-find-a-job book but rather helps you in your job search by making you smarter. Smarter is good, because the Net Economy is a meritocracy. You won't be able to get by on anything else. *Internet Jobs!* shows you how much the world of work has changed since it collided with the Internet. *Internet Jobs!* describes the world you will inhabit.

In other words, *Internet Jobs!* is not about how to get a Net job, but about what Net jobs there are to get. There are many books about the process of getting a job, including writing resumes for the Net, networking, using the Internet search engines, interviewing, and negotiating. These are indispensable skills, and I encourage you to master them. But first you might want to better understand the emerging world of Net jobs. If that is your goal, welcome aboard.

Preface

YOU'RE IN LUCK

The entire world is moving to the Internet, and it needs you to help with the heavy lifting. You are on the ground floor of a massive transformation that historians will look back on as every bit as significant as the Industrial Revolution. And here's the best part. It turns out that this new revolution—let's call it the Net Economy—needs you as much as you need it. We encourage you to take the attitude that the Net Economy cannot take place without you. If you think this attitude is the height of arrogance—that the Net Economy is bigger than any individual—you'd be right. You'd also be at a disadvantage for a meaningful career in the Net Economy. Net-ready organizations need people with attitude as much as they need people with technical skills. This book will describe both the attitude and technical skills you will need.

Take a good look around. The Internet is here and in a few short years has surprisingly infiltrated the infrastructure of the Western countries. The rest of the world will overtake us in a year or so. The predominant language on the Net right now is English. That will change before we are ready. Language notwithstanding, the Net is remarkably standardized. The bits and bytes and practices and etiquette that underlie the Net have been largely commoditized. The technology wars have been won. The task at hand is getting the job done. That requires filling positions with people who bring a portfolio of skills, experience, and attitude.

That said, the Internet is an infrastructure in progress. It's dominated by the very bright people who built it. Technology will continue to have an indispensable role in the evolution of the Internet, but this book suggests that it would be a mistake to give short shrift to the opportunities presented by the unrelenting demand for content. The Internet will continue to need people with skills in writing, video, animation, illustration, photography, and music. Eventually, as we will show, the opportunities in the content area will eclipse those generated by the need for more infrastructure.

All of these people and resources will have to be managed. One of the myths of the Net culture is that cyberspace is self-managing. We know that is not the case. The Net is a human artifact, and it needs as much management as any other human activity—and by virtue of its real-time nature, maybe more. The Net will continue to require people who can manage the relationships between vision, money, technology, and art.

GOOD NEWS AND BAD NEWS

For people who have a critical mass of talent for generating content, technical skills, management savvy, and attitude, the prospects are unlimited. That's at once the good news and the bad news.

The good news is that there are more opportunities than you can possibly choose from.   is

The bad news is that there are more opportunities than you can possibly choose from.

This paradox drives many smart and ambitious people crazy. Whether the abundance of choice leaves you flush with excitement or paralyzed with indecision will determine your fitness for service in the Net Economy. This book will offer you some advice on how to manage expectations in a world of unlimited opportunity.

In the unforgiving calculus of the Internet job market, too many opportunities are indistinguishable from too few. Given the pace of change in the Net Economy, how are you going to choose? Do you want a career in the private or public sector? Start-up or established company? Born-on-the-Web organization or one with roots in the traditional economy? Large or small? Domestic or international? What skill sets do you need? Do you specialize or generalize? Will you provide content or manage infrastructure? Do you want to be a full-time employee or a contract worker? Do you want to work in an office setting or telecommute? The questions, like the opportunities, are endless.

NETJOBS.COM

There is an accelerated quality about the Net. It compresses time and demands immediacy and interactivity. A book, such as the one you are holding in your hand, is not the ideal medium to describe this new domain. Things happen too fast and change even faster. Any specific information—salaries, specific positions, college recruitment promotions, job fairs—that this book might offer will be long irrelevant by the time you read this. Nevertheless, a printed book has advantages. It doesn't need batteries. You can read it on the bus on the way to a job interview. You can give it to a friend.

For that reason, you will find an *Internet Jobs!* Web site that includes the links to the resources described in the book. The *Internet Jobs!* Web site will also be updated with the latest statistics and salary information. I hope you will use the Web site in association with the printed book to further your understanding of the issues and increase the depth of your perspective about the world of Internet jobs. Point your browser to *www.jkador.com/netjobs.*

A PERSONAL NOTE

As a freelance writer, I have been a member of the contingent workforce for over 17 years. I became an independent writer in the same way that every other freelance writer, without exception, in the entire history of the world assumed that honor: I was fired from a full-time job.

Getting fired from the advertising agency where I worked as a copywriter was the best thing that ever happened to me.

Okay, so at the time my perspective was slightly different. All I remember of those first days is the fervent hope that maybe someday I would live in a universe where anxiety, depression, and panic were attractive qualities.

But as time went on and my writing assignments became more stable, I realized just what a gift my former boss gave me. For the past 17 years, I made much more money than I ever would have as a staff member of the ad agency. More importantly, I got to pick my assignments. No more writing brochures on sludge aspirators. I could work when I wanted to, and I didn't have to commute. Best of all, I could stay at home and be with my children when they got home from school.

Not that I was chained to my desk. In the course of my assignments, I got to visit hundreds of companies all around the world. Sometimes I became friendly with the most senior executives. Other times my contacts were with people in the data center. As I talked to these people, I realized that every job is being transformed by the Internet. At the same time, I was privileged to have direct contact with a number of colleges and universities and a number of people in the entry phase of their careers. I saw how the Net is transforming their prospects.

Looking back, I see that my success is a function of equal doses of luck and pluck. I had the good fortune of being set loose on the ground floor of the biggest economic miracle in the history of the world. It was 1983 and the PC revolution was exploding. The trade magazines needed unlimited volumes of editorial material to separate the advertisements. The hardware and software companies needed brochures, speeches, and white papers. I was ready, and my career took off.

I also developed some writing practices and personal philosophies that kept the assignments flowing. Here are a few reasons I believe I have been successful:

- If I said you'll have it Thursday, you'll have it Thursday. I learned that clients would rather have it on time and good enough than late and perfect.

- I knew when good enough is good enough. Writing projects are never finished; they are only abandoned. I knew when to abandon them so I could move on to the next assignment.

- I cultivated relationships. All business is ultimately about personal relationships. I went out of my way to get to know my clients on a personal basis. I didn't have to. All transactions could have been handled via phone, fax, or e-mail. But every year, I made it a point to visit, have lunch, and ask them what their challenges were for the next period. I made friends and always walked away with more assignments.

- I trained myself to multitask. Success is a function of keeping a number of projects in the air at one time.

- I invested in my own development. I took advantage of every training opportunity to learn about new technologies, processes, architectures, and business models.

Now it's time for you to move your career forward in the Net Economy. I wish you the best in all your endeavors.

John Kador
Geneva, IL
August 1999

Acknowledgments

I have been blessed with the assistance of many colleagues and friends in the writing of *Internet Jobs!* A book such as this displaces a lot of love and patience. Fortunately, my life is endowed with unlimited quantities of both. I want to thank my family for encouraging me even when I wasn't available for family pursuits. As always, Anna Beth, Daniel, and Rachel supported me in the tangible and intangible ways families do.

For reading the manuscript and making invaluable suggestions, I am grateful to Alan Farber, Coordinator of Career Services, Counseling, and Student Development Center, Northern Illinois University; Bob Levy; and Rich Seeley.

I am indebted to two members in good standing of the contingent workforce for assisting me in the preparation of this manuscript. Rita Hoover, as diligent a friend as she is a writer, assembled the chapter on the 100 Hottest Companies on the Net. Rita, a newspaper columnist and freelance writer, is based in Geneva, Illinois. The husband and wife writing team of Richard Seeley and Peggy Radcliffe, based in Palm Springs, California, did all the content aggregation for the 50 Hottest Net Cities chapter.

Thanks also to Amir Hartman and John Sifonis, my co-authors on *Net Ready: Strategies for Success in the E-conomy*, for their many courtesies. *Internet Jobs!* was written simultaneously with *Net Ready*, a fact that could have inspired conflict but produced synergy. Some of the conclusions of *Net Ready* (also published by McGraw-Hill) inform chapter 2 of this book. Readers who want two examples of how to take charge of a career, how to brand oneself, and how to navigate between full-time and contingent employment have but to look to Messrs. Hartman and Sifonis for direction.

This book would have been impossible without the generous contributions of a number of busy people who responded to my increasingly desperate pleas for help on various Internet discussion lists. My thanks go to: Aiden Barr, Deborah Coughlin, Kelly Dingee, David Dircks, Beth Fleischer, Gerri Garvin,

Bob Gordon, David Howard, Mike Iserson, Linda Jacobson, Matthew Jure, Christa Kennis, Carie Lemack, Bill Little, Pat Loomis, Sara McKiness, Derrek Milan, Danielle Monaghan, Jeff Pidgeon, Sean Rolinson, Velda Ruddock, Stan E. Settle, Margaret Steen, Dr. John Sullivan, Martin Tobias, Susan Trainer, Annette Wagner, Julie Wallof, Tom Wong, and James R. Ziegler, PhD.

At McGraw-Hill, I owe many thanks, in particular to my editor, Betsy Brown, for entrusting me with this project.

Finally, there remains one last group of people to name. I am blessed with a team of friends who have been at the center of every project I have taken on in the past decade. This book is in no small measure a product of their unconditional commitment to my success. I am honored to be called a friend by Rita Hoover, George Moskoff, Ryia Ross, Stephanie Simmons Ray, Taylor McMaster, Laura Vasilion, Steve Vasilion, and Mary Wang.

Introduction

THE INTERNET GOLD RUSH OF THE TWENTY-FIRST CENTURY

If you were alive during the California gold rush of 1849, would you stay on your farm in Kansas or would you immediately pack up and start digging for the golden opportunity? If you were 18 during the final years of the 1960s, wouldn't you kick yourself every day for missing the original Woodstock Music Festival?

Well, in the twenty-first century the opportunity that you will regret missing is a job in the new Internet economy! Many people mistakenly believe that the way to get rich in the Internet revolution is by investing in Internet stocks. That might work from time to time, but to create real wealth on a sustainable basis, you'll be better off by getting an Internet job and becoming a permanent part of the Net economy.

The Internet and e-commerce create more dramatic opportunities than the California goal rush ever did! People who are now starting their careers and those who are considering changing jobs have a unique opportunity that should not be passed up.

As was the case during the California gold rush, there are no guaranteed maps that will lead you directly to success. It will take some effort and self-education on your part in order to be successful in the Internet economy. With so many opportunities available, one of the biggest challenges is to decide what opportunity you want. In this book you'll find enough ideas and tips so that you can successfully navigate your way to a great job in the brave new world of the Internet!

Early in this book you will learn about the Internet economy and how it is changing the world of business. You will learn about opportunities in e-commerce, the Internet, and the new world of work. In the Internet economy, change occurs at a dizzying pace. Products are produced on a just-in-time basis and then mass-customized to fit the individual needs of individual customers. Traditional business processes such as marketing, accounting, inventory control, and product design perpetually become "faster, cheaper, and better." If there is a theoretical limit to this trend, its horizon is not visible as of yet. By the same token, opportunities for those with "outside-the-box" ideas and those willing to take risks will be limitless.

The Net revolution will shift power toward those with the skills necessary to navigate the new economy. Because there is and there will continue to be a dramatic shortage of Net talent, those who possess the right portfolio of skills will be in the driver's seat. As the Net economy expands, it will also offer unprecedented opportunities for those with new ideas and new ways of thinking.

However, there will also be burdens. Individuals will need to continuously update their skills and intellectual capital as new technologies develop. Whatever you learned in school will rapidly become obsolete. Successful individuals will no longer be able to limit their knowledge to a single technical or business area. As the barrier between having technical knowledge and understanding the business model blurs, employees will need both sets of skills in order to excel. Successful individuals in the Net economy will develop a deep and seamless understanding of the interoperations of hardware and software and the customer-focused business model that they support.

Participants in the Net economy have a dizzying array of choices of how and when they work. The Net gives applicants abundant choices regarding the type of employment that is available to them. Instead of traditional nine-to-five jobs, there will be a wide variety of options including contract work, consulting, part-time work, work at home, project work, and an ever-exploding combination of these.

Candidates entering the job market today find a variety of opportunities for internships, externships, part-time work, and on-the-job apprenticeship programs that will make it easier to develop the skills needed to get ahead. It is essential, however, that you understand the advantages and disadvantages of each of these models and the opportunities they enable. These are extremely volatile models. As you prepare yourself for your new career, be especially wary of outdated materials and advisers who may with all good intentions lead you astray.

In addition to understanding how the economy works, it is equally important for the applicant to understand what jobs will be available, what skills these jobs will require, and what steps one should take to prepare for these jobs. As *Internet Jobs!* so ably explains, net-enabled jobs can be categorized into three areas:

- The first is content development. Here you may be writing programs, developing software, or you could be designing the content of Web pages. These are exciting jobs, which offer an opportunity to be creative and to work in an unstructured team environment. Many of these jobs do not require extensive technical backgrounds and as a result people from the liberal and creative arts can be just as successful as those from science and engineering.

- The second category of jobs are infrastructure or hardware-related jobs. Here there are tremendous opportunities to develop hardware, build networks, maintain network security, and become a Webmaster.

- The third segment of job opportunities is in the business or operations area. As e-commerce develops, finance skills will become essential if firms are to sell their products and services over the Web. Marketing and public relations skills are an integral part of both getting people to visit your Web site and in getting them to purchase goods and services from you. Because e-commerce is an evolving field, successful applicants need new skills, which cannot always be obtained through traditional experience or even education.

It is essential that applicants for Net jobs understand their unique skill requirements so that they can laser focus their skill development in the areas that will have the most impact in preparing them for these exciting new job opportunities.

In addition to knowing about the job opportunities it is equally important for any entrant into this field to know about the best places to work. What makes a company a great place to work? Must it be a born-on-the-Web enterprise or can a traditional firm with a strong Web presence be equally as attractive? Applicants need to know what the characteristics of a great job are, how to find out about the appropriate levels of pay and benefits, and even about the stock options. Individuals making a shift to net-related jobs also need to understand the advantages of working for smaller firms that may go through an IPO. Applicants who are considering relocation should also be aware of the fastest-growing geographic areas where net-related firms are located. Getting any job is not enough; the goal is to get the right job, at the right firm, and with the appropriate rewards!

As a professor over the past two decades, I have had the opportunity to study, visit, and consult with the best firms in the Silicon Valley and elsewhere. My students have seen me go from recommending Internet and hi-tech jobs to a laser focus close to insistence. "You are crazy if you don't try them first" is the subtext of my current advice. Because these firms offer recent college grads such outstanding opportunities to apply their "out-of-the-box" ideas with a minimum of bureaucracy, they offer the most attractive work environments I am aware of. Incidentally, the management style and practices of these firms are the envy of other managers and, truth be told, professors.

It's time to wake up. Don't miss the 21st century gold rush...the Internet job rush! Stop looking for just "any job." Instead, begin preparing for *the* opportunity of the 21st century. Begin now and get in on the ground floor, be-cause, as history demonstrates over and over again, there are always limits on limitless opportunities.

Dr. John Sullivan
Head and Professor of Human Resources
College of Business
San Francisco State University, California
December 1999

PART 1
Net-Enabled Careers

Making the Internet indispensable and relevant to every person and every business, every day.

—Microsoft's new mission statement
for the Net Economy

NO TIME FOR JOBS

It's tempting to think of careers in terms of jobs—roles that are approximated by job titles and neatly characterized by job descriptions. The reality in the Net Economy is that organizations have no time for people who insist on just doing their jobs. Job descriptions in the Net Economy typically define the minimal expectations, technical and otherwise, that the person should have. The Internet is far too fluid and dynamic for anything more specific. It is the kiss of death in the Net Economy for a worker to invoke a job description in an effort to limit his or her involvement. Job descriptions should be seen as a jumping-off point.

Successful workers in the Net Economy have a high tolerance for ambiguity. If you have a need for a title and job description written in permanent ink, look elsewhere. Successful workers in the Net Economy are eager to jump into new challenges. Successful companies are eager to have their employees take on new challenges, learning as they go.

This book is designed to assist people entering the job market to identify the career opportunities in the rapidly expanding worlds of the digital economy, Web publishing, and e-commerce. The book describes the technical and non-technical positions that are offered by digital-economy companies across the spectrum of enterprises. It further offers information about what these employers require in the way of skills and what they offer in return.

The goal of the first section of *Internet Jobs!* is to set the stage for the specific careers that the Net Economy has created.

Chapter 1 describes how the Net has changed all our assumptions about work and careers. One big change is that you are a brand of one. Manage your brand, because no one else will.

In chapter 2, you'll be introduced to ten powerful trends shaping the Net Economy.

Full-time or part-time? Chapter 3 discusses the rise of the contingency workforce and lays out the advantages of working as a free agent.

1
New Worlds of Work

There always comes a moment in time when a door opens
and lets the future in.

—Graham Greene

Amazing things happen when work collides with the Web. Everything we have ever learned about work from watching TV or watching our parents turns out to be irrelevant. The most basic concepts of work—jobs, time, loyalty, compensation, and experiences—have been permanently redefined.

In a fundamentally new way, the Web offers the possibility of connecting us to our jobs. It reconnects jobs to what matters to people: creativity, meaning, responsibility, and humanity. By bringing buyers and sellers together, by rendering irrelevant the tyranny of time and space, the Web allows people to express their creativity, create wealth, and do it with a level of personal power, responsibility, and authority that has not been seen since humans invented the plow and domesticated beasts of burden.

In this process, well-accepted beliefs and assumptions about the nature of work and business have been turned topsy-turvy. Most of all, the Web has completely transformed the balance of power between employees and employers, buyers and sellers, organizations and individuals. In every case, the Web has shifted the balance of power. Today employees, buyers, and individuals call the shots.

MORE POWER TO EMPLOYEES

Concentrations of capital, raw materials, and transportation channels fuel the growth of industrial organizations. E-Businesses are fueled by one thing only: creative, talented people. E-Business leaders know that people can go anywhere, which means that their biggest challenge isn't the competition for products. It's the competition for human resources. The number one competency for companies such as Microsoft or Computer Associates International is recruitment and retention.

Are you a talented, creative person? Guess what? That means the balance of power has shifted to your side. You may not know it, but it's a fact. You get to exercise a degree of personal autonomy in your job search and career that is absolutely unprecedented. Let's assume you have the right combination of talent, competencies, and attitude. In a seller's market for talent, you get to shop for the right boss, the right colleagues, and the right environment. In the old economy, it was a buyer's market. Enterprises had more people than slots, and the question they asked was "Why should we hire you?" In the Net Economy, there are more opportunities searching for talented people, and there are no slots anymore. Now the question is, "What else can we tell you so you will lend us your allegiance?"

MORE POWER TO BUYERS

For a number of reasons, the Net Economy shifts the balance of power from sellers to buyers. Buyers are increasingly calling the shots, from telling sellers what their products are worth to dictating the way the sellers format their catalogs. Most of all, consumers expect to be presented with the highest levels of operational excellence. They insist on being treated as valued partners and as discerning members of a community in which they have a right to be well informed.

Companies soon saw that the Net catalyzed a change from the one-to-many relationships corporations knew to a new world of one-to-one customer management. It suddenly became possible for companies such as Cisco Systems and Charles Schwab to manage unique relationships with each of its customers. That possibility, in turn, changed many transactional relationships into transformational relationships, characterized by an aligning of interests that would have been thought impossible a few years earlier. Enterprises such as Onsale and eBay are representative of firms exploiting one-to-one transformative relationships.

At the same time, the Net Economy redefines every assumption about dealing with customers. Consider the strategy of customer relationship management (CRM). The Net Economy will throw this well-intentioned but unworkable management discipline on its ears. That's because with Net-ready customers having so many options to choose from in any product or service category, it is most certainly not the customer who's being managed. That's way too passive. In the Net Economy, it's the customer who gets to manage the relationship. Net-readiness requires organizations to let go of the arrogance of assuming that customers and clients can be manipulated. In the Net Economy, customers can only be served, listened to, and valued. Then, if the company does everything right, the customer may agree to be served.

The Web allows individuals to reclaim their power. Organizations and the economies of scale they commanded used to put individuals at a grave disadvantage in any transaction. No longer. The Web does two main things. First it levels out the asymmetries of information that kept power in the hands of large enterprises. Second, it disembowels the notion of mass production and mass marketing, concepts that sucked power from individuals. Look for opportunities that exploit one-to-one relationships and mass customization.

SHOW ME THE MONEY!

Money has always been important to employees and business. Yet in the traditional economy, there is a stupefying level of pretense about money. Even though it's the first thing on the mind of the candidates ("How much money can I get?"), and it's the first thing on the minds of the executives doing the hiring ("How much money will I have to pay?"), money is the absolute last item on the agenda. Does that make sense?

The Web, happily, dismantles some of the pretense. Critics call the new generation of workers greedy, selfish, and in it only for what they can get. Absolutely true, just as it's always been. Only now we have the decency to acknowledge it. And the funny thing is, the more we acknowledge it, the less it is true. It turns out that once we have a frank conversation about money, are offered what we are worth, and get it out of the way, other things begin to take on as much or more importance. Learning opportunities. More training. Cool people to work with. Personal autonomy. All these can and do become more important than money.

However, the conversation about money comes first. And for talented people with Web savvy, what a conversation it is. Money talks, and it's on speaking terms with Web talent. The Net Economy is simply, or perhaps not so simply, awash in money. Venture capitalists are pouring funds into startups at a stupendous rate. In 1999, for example, venture-capital firms raised over $15 billion. More than 750 companies went public, with a total valuation of over $50 billion. The lion's share of that money goes for one thing: talent to create intellectual property. In other words, it goes to software. And you are the software. Most of that money is designed to get you to create, maintain, market, and support the assets that create value for the investors.

For most Web wannabees, the name of the game is not salary but stock options. Chalk it up as another legacy of Microsoft and that company's now-legendary cadre of millionaires. Across the landscape of the new economy, young, well-educated, talented businesspeople are joining up to get a piece of the action. They're willing to forgo larger salaries at bigger and better-established firms in favor of stock options in upstarts that may be worth a great deal down the road. The result: Even small, little-known enterprises can compete for top talent. In fact, startups promising high risk and huge gain are winning.

CONTINUOUS LEARNING

If there's anything more important to Web people than money, it's the opportunity to learn new technologies, processes, and business skills. Technical people recognize they cannot advance without business skills. Business people acknowledge they need a better understanding of technology in order to be successful. Both camps strive for that crucial balance between technical and business skills and demand a variety of training and educational opportunities to meet that need.

The most successful Web companies have figured out what it takes to succeed in a knowledge-based economy. Learning becomes the coin of the realm. These companies know that talented people join up in order to learn. Of course, part of the attraction of learning is linked to money. Learn more today, earn more tomorrow. But many Web people, especially those focused on technology, seek out the intellectual challenge more than the money. They like being equipped with the latest tools as they explore the frontiers of the knowledge economy. They appreciate the opportunity to work with the coolest people, use the most advanced tools, empowered by the best training in the latest skills. Companies have heard the message. They want to hire people who maintain their hunger to learn and respond by creating an environment where such people are presented with opportunities for continuous learning.

BRAND YOURSELF

We surround ourselves with brands. We love brands. Think Nike. Think Starbucks. Think Martha Stewart. Think "Intel Inside." Brands put us at ease because we have confidence in them. And we are happy to pay for that confidence. A brand is something customers will pay extra for, even if it's on a product or service identical to a competitor's.

The implication is clear: brand yourself. Create a compelling value proposition that unmistakably brands you in the exact way that will move your agenda forward. When you have a personal brand, employers will pay something extra for you even if they have a lower-cost alternative. This is exactly what you want.

Businesses create wealth by transforming commodities into products and then into brands. Consider Nike. They took footwear from a commodity (sneakers) to a product (running shoes) and then a brand (Nike athletic shoes with the swoosh coordinated with every other imaginable product). If you have been to a Niketown store, you know that Nike is well on its way to transcending brand by turning Nike into an experience. People are willing to pay more for experiences than for products, even branded products The lesson is that you can increase your value to the extent that you can transform an employer's perception of you into an experience.

If you are serious about taking yourself seriously, you should be reading a powerful new magazine called *Fast Company* (www.fastcompany.com). This publication is Exhibit A of the branded, self-actualized, free agent of the Web Economy. *Fast Company*'s major contribution to the employment theory is popularizing the argument that every member of the Net Economy should treat himself or herself as a brand. And that means that career planning becomes brand management.

To build a brand, start by asking the same question the brand managers at Coke or McDonald's ask themselves:

- What is it that my product or service offers that would make people pay extra for it?

Before you answer that, it might be useful for you to consider a number of other questions brand managers have learned to ask themselves. In the context of promoting yourself as a candidate, much as Proctor & Gamble promotes one of its brands, ask yourself:

- What are the qualities and characteristics that make me distinctive from my competitors?
- What have I done lately to make myself stand out? (And by "lately," think "this week.")
- What do I want to be famous for?
- What do I consider my greatest and most noteworthy trait?
- How would my favorite professor or manager answer the same question?
- How would my greatest enemy or competitor answer the same question?
- What can I do that adds remarkable, measurable, distinguished, and distinctive value?

It's not about degrees, credentials, job descriptions, or titles anymore. It's about what you can deliver—or, by virtue of other things you have done, what you can demonstrate that you will deliver. What have you accomplished that you can unabashedly brag about? No one else is going to brag about it if you don't. If you are going to be a brand, you've got to become relentlessly focused on what you do that adds value, that you're proud of, and most important, that you can shamelessly take credit for.

So let's have that question again.

- What is it that my product or service offers that would make people pay extra for it?

This is such an important question that I invite you to take a minute to reflect on how you would answer it in fifteen words or less. You can't assume you'll get more than fifteen words out before they lose attention, so limit your answer to fifteen words or less, please. Take the time to write your answer in the following space.

_____

_____

There is only one way to know if the branding statement you settled on is good or not. You have to test it. If your answer does not light up the eyes of an interviewer or prospective supervisor, if it does not command a vote of confidence from a professor who knows your work, then you have a problem. It means you have to give some critical consideration to imagining and developing yourself as a brand.

ROLES THAT ADD VALUE

Realize that your career is a function of your ability to add value to whatever team, project, or organization that happens to hold your allegiance. You will always be measured by how much value you add. There are six roles in the Net Economy that will serve you. Make sure your personal mission statement accommodates as many of these roles as possible:

1. Be a businessperson. Business is not a dirty word. If you can't be proud of it, you have no business being there. Know the business. Be obsessed with pragmatic outcomes.

2. Be a leader. Let go of the discredited notion that some people are leaders and others are followers. Everyone gets to lead something sometime. Back into leadership if you have to. Start by being a teacher, a role model, a mentor. Graduate to being a visionary. Pretty soon you will have people following you. You're suddenly a leader. Don't act too surprised. Leaders are not appointed. They earn it.

3. Be a team player. Work in the Net Economy is organized in teams. If you are not perceived as a great teammate and supportive colleague, you will get only as far as the limits of your own knowledge and talent. It won't be enough.

4. Be a world class expert in something. Maybe it's a quality process, a dialect of Unix, a software application, or a strategic planning discipline. You've got to be seen as an available and enthusiastic resource.

5. Be wired. Know the ins and outs of the Net and Web technologies. Strive to integrate every process with the Web. Use it as a collaborative platform across all your professional interactions and relationships.

6. Be obsessed with customer service. We all have customers to serve. Ask yourself, "To whom do I owe information?" They are your customers. Get to know them and what they want. If you're not sure, ask them. If you are sure, ask them anyway.

2
Net Economy Rules

The race doesn't always go to the swift,
nor the battle to the strong,
but that's the way to bet.

—Anonymous

THE NET ECONOMY

If your goal is to get a job in the Net Economy, it's good to get a good grasp of the rules or principles by which the Net Economy operates. This chapter articulates a few of those rules.

While it's elusive to pin down a definition of the Net Economy, its operating principles are a little easier to describe. You'll always be better off choosing job or project opportunities that are aligned with the strategic movement of the Net Economy. If you can get ahead of the curve, so much the better. So if you understand the following principles of the Net Economy, you will be in a much better position to identify and define job or project opportunities that fit your mission statement and can leverage the tectonic movements of this environment.

First, let's define the Net Economy:

The virtual arena in which business actually is conducted, value is created and exchanged, transactions occur, and one-to-one relationships mature. These processes may be related to, but are nevertheless independent of, similar activities occurring in the conventional marketplace.

The Net Economy, with its relentlessly real-time attributes, demands a new mindset to embrace it. As it imposes a new order, the old industrial view of the world is found to be wholly inadequate to the task of understanding and anticipating the opportunities created by the Net Economy. The most difficult struggle is to forget definitions and practices that we have already learned. The hardest thing in the world is to give up practices that have made us rich. Yet this is exactly what success in the Net Economy demands.

TEN TRENDS OF THE NET ECONOMY

To date, the traditional economy has emphasized the manufacture and distribution of tangible goods and services. This emphasis on static attributes of supply and demand is changing faster than our ability to describe it. Nevertheless, let's try to articulate some of the strategic shifts the Net Economy imposes on those who would exploit it.

Every period of human history has been organized by sets of economic forces that have eventually yielded to new sets of forces. Before humans understood the principles of agriculture, hunting-and-gathering economies dominated the world. The principles of hunting and gathering were simple and perfectly understood: people consumed what they hunted or gathered and then moved on. Economic planning, such as it was, restricted itself to considerations about the next meal.

The information era replaced the industrial age at some amorphous point in the 1950s. At first, the economics and assumptions of the industrial economy limited the possibilities of information processing. Computers were big, centralized machines locked in glass-walled rooms to do long division under the ministrations of a new priesthood called MIS. The computers attacked back-office operations such as sorting and collating. They were administered by technicians with their own language who promoted the idea that computers were complicated and somehow dangerous, like a blast furnace or refinery. It was only with the PC revolution in the early 1980s that the information economy was put into the hands of end users who, taking advantage of "insanely great" tools such as the Apple Macintosh, changed the world in an incredibly short period of time.

The Internet, finally, ties the industrial and information economies together to create the Net Economy, an environment with a brand new set of operating principles underscored by a whole new set of economic realities. The more you understand these principles and use them to leverage your job search, the more focused your agenda can be. Map the opportunities that are presented to you against these trends. The Net can deliver impressive rewards or undermine ambitious plans. It's up to you to be on the winning side of the equation. Ensuring that the positions you choose are aligned with these trends doesn't guarantee success. But choosing a position that goes against the grain of these trends dooms any initiative. The ten trends are:

○ Web Master
○ Web page design
○ Database Admin
○ E-Commerce
○

○ Lan\ Network Engineer
○ Technician
○

1. Net jobs advance either <u>content</u> or <u>infrastructure.</u>
2. Industries are shifting from static to dynamic as products and services mutate from tangible to intangible.
3. Customization: Customers are becoming less forgiving and more discerning.
4. New infomediaries are extracting value.
5. Convergence: Value chains are becoming more integrated.
6. Digitization: Electronic relationships are emerging.
7. Informatization: Smart products are proliferating.
8. Compression: Transaction costs are being slashed.
9. Time is money: Why speed matters.
10. Advantage is becoming more temporary.

There is no status quo. Every day is a new competitive arena, and the pace of change is now running at Internet speed. Consider the ways internal business structures, industry boundaries, and customer outcomes and expectations morph when subject to the vagaries of the Net Economy. Do the attributes of the enterprises or opportunities you are considering align with the traditional economy or the Net Economy? Add it up. If the score comes down too far to the left, you are playing with the deck stacked against you.

1. Net Jobs Advance Either Content or Infrastructure

All jobs in the Internet fall into one of two major classifications: content and infrastructure. It's useful to understand how the Net combines content and infrastructure to create value. You can improve your chances of finding a rewarding career by being clear on which side of the content-infrastructure continuum you want to be. Let's define our terms.

Content is commonly understood to be the "message" in Marshall McLuhan's famous dictum, "the medium is the message." On the most granular level, content is anything that people create to impart information. Commonly it takes the forms of writing, illustration, animation, music, video, photography, and other graphic or multimedia representations of the human experience. But let's define content from a more abstract and powerful perspective:

> Information, data, experience, or knowledge that provides a framework for action. Examples include books, articles, software, music, and instructions. Any time you generate information, data, methods, knowledge, or wisdom in any form—print, broadcast, text, or multimedia—you are creating content.

This definition suits our purposes better because it underscores the deep opportunities in the Net Economy for people to generate, edit, revise, assemble, and otherwise manipulate content.

Balancing the concept of content in this discussion is the concept of infrastructure:

> The framework by which content is transformed, accessed, delivered, or applied. Examples include networks, LANs, PCs, printers, CD players, and cameras.

The Net Economy creates exciting opportunities for those who recognize that the Net is transforming traditional concepts of products and services into new measures of economic value in terms of content and infrastructure. If an organization wants to make significant money in the Net Economy, it must provide a compelling proposition that adds value either to the content or the infrastructure. The traditional marketplace makes a durable distinction between content providers and infrastructure providers. It's generally either one or the other, and it can be traumatic for people and organizations to be forced to migrate from one to the other. For example, in the traditional economy, you can either be a content provider, such as a book writer, or an infrastructure provider, such as a publisher. It's rare to be both. But in the Net Economy, the distinctions between the two strategic areas are much more slippery and dynamic. Today, it is common for writers to use the attributes of the Net to publish their work. The essence of competing in the Net Economy is a function of the nimbleness a company displays in navigating the relationship between content and infrastructure.

In general, infrastructure jobs are most appealing in the earliest stages of deployment of an architecture. This is when innovation and value are at their highest. For example, a job building America Online's infrastructure probably paid off big-time in terms of stock options. Today America Online is squarely a media company, more attentive to acquiring content and "eyeballs" (a combination nicely provided by Netscape) than creating new infrastructure. AOL offers jobs in both areas, but in which area do you think your career would advance most? At this point in the evolution of the Net Economy, most of the juice has been squeezed out of building infrastructure. Now it's mostly deployment, maintenance, and incremental design. Revolutionary developments are more likely on the content end of the spectrum.

2. Industries Are Shifting from Static to Dynamic as Products and Services Mutate from Tangible to Intangible

By eradicating the distinctions between global and local businesses, the Net Economy shifts industrial boundaries from the static to the dynamic. The result is global competition of a uniquely furious and unpredictable nature. Enterprises that formerly competed or partnered in different spaces now find themselves confronting each other.

Our lives are filled with examples of the mutation of formerly tangible products and services to intangible ones. The process is often so seamless and natural as to be transparent. This is a process as old as humanity. At first there was barter, a mutual exchange of tangibles. Money, with all the benefits of intangibility, quickly replaced barter. Today, electronic commerce is turning the country into a cashless economy. So the process is hardly new, just accelerated. Here are just a few examples:

- E-Tickets. We used to make a trip to the travel agent, where we received a paper airplane ticket, which we presented to the boarding agent. Today, we visit a Web site and receive an e-ticket and a PIN that lets us generate a boarding pass from a kiosk at the gate.
- Software Sales. We used to distribute software on tangible diskettes or CDs. Increasingly, software is downloaded from Web sites.
- Reference Works. We used to visit libraries to consult tangible reference works—encyclopedias, dictionaries, almanacs. Increasingly, these resources are available online, always accessible and always up-to-date.

Where do the opportunities that you are considering fall on the tangible-intangible continuum?

3. Customization: Customers Are Becoming Less Forgiving and More Discerning

Mass customization is the organizing principle of business in the Net Economy, just as mass production was the organizing principle of the traditional economy. Mass producers dictate a one-to-many relationship. Mass customizers take advantage of information technologies that create the type of products and services that cannot be compared to a competitor's. Why? Because each product and service is unique, as a result of an ongoing, one-on-one dialogue with each of its customers. The results often take our breath away. We all know about Dell, a company that has a one-on-one relationship with customers, both companies and individuals, and builds only PCs that have actually been ordered. The range of possibilities for Net Economy entities built around customization are limitless.

Customization allows organizations the power to give every customer a unique view of the organization. Services such as "My Yahoo!" or "My eBay" allow each user to configure a unique relationship with the company, based on the unique interests and desires of the customer. Millions of people have not only the illusion, but the reality, of a customized encounter. A core theme of customization is the assumption that everyone should have the equivalent of a My Yahoo! across the spectrum of products and services. Consumers increasingly want more power to produce what they consume. In that way, each of us strives to create a unique and custom-tailored point of encounter with the parties that supply products and services for our personal consumption. In the Net Economy, every company should consider this concept as an invitation—no, a demand!—to create a "personalized" version of their product or service offering.

The Net Economy also eliminates asymmetries of information. In other words, it promotes a transactional environment in which every buyer and seller has perfect information. The Net Economy can no longer sustain enterprises whose value proposition assumes better information than the next guy. Look at the opportunities presented to you. Do they give each customer an individual value proposition? Do they take advantage of a world of perfect information? If so, they are with the grain of the Net Economy.

4. New Infomediaries Are Extracting Value

One of the most durable myths of the Net Economy is that the Web systematically eliminates all infomediaries by squeezing out of the economy the inefficiencies that middlemen such as brokers now exploit. *Disintermediation,* a nice piece of jargon, refers to the eradication of a layer or function that exists between two other layers or functions. There's just one problem: it's not going to happen. At least not in the way some experts believe. While some infomediaries may disappear, the very nature of the Web opens up new niches to add value. Companies quick and agile enough to detect opportunities in complex markets will prosper as infomediaries. The new niches thus created are part of the value web. If you can find a niche, you can be a storefront in a new value web.

Wait a minute, you say. What about all those celebrated examples of disintermediation that we've read about in *Business Week?* Doesn't Amazon eliminate the layer between consumer and bookseller? The answer is an unequivocal "no." Although Amazon has changed the way certain segments of the market consume books, it is a case of a new channel replacing old channels, not disintermediation. Amazon is a perfect example of how the Web has added another value-added retail channel. Real disintermediation occurs when Viking, McGraw-Hill, or Random House start making a major effort to sell their books directly to consumers. While it's possible to order books directly from the Websites of publishers such as McGraw-Hill or Prentice Hall, the orders are processed through an infomediary, a book dealer transparent to the buyer, but nevertheless an infomediary. Similarly, Amazon uses a book distributor to fulfill its distribution services. Amazon offers customers many compelling benefits, but they are not in the area of disintermediation.

Don't be concerned if the initiative you are offered acts as an infomediary. Well-considered infomediaries are poised to transform every industry, from travel to insurance to real estate.

5. Convergence: Value Chains Are Becoming More Integrated

Convergence describes the phenomenon of two or more existing technologies, markets, producers, boundaries, or value chains combining to create a new force that is more powerful and more efficient than the sum of its parts. Convergence is not a new dynamic; it has been going on as long as human beings have been developing and refining technologies, roles, and markets.

The outcome of any significant convergence is never really predictable. People sometimes believe that convergence operates by combining technology A with technology B and getting some hybrid that has some reasonably obvious elements of both. But that's not the way convergence works. When the technologies of the automobile and road building converged to create the interstate highway system, no one could have predicted the massive social disruptions—from fast food to population shifts—that a mobile society created. In the same way, when the technologies of radio and cinema converged to create television, no one could have predicted the unifying and disconnecting forces that we still do not fully understand today. The law of unintended consequences has a field day whenever significant technologies converge.

Deconstruct the opportunity before you to see how it exploits convergence. The more powerful the forces that are converging, the more opportunities there may be.

6. Digitization: Electronic Relationships Are Emerging

In the simplest sense, digitization refers to representing content in ones and zeros, the language of computers. But the ability to represent content—text, video, audio, images—in this way opens up the door to unprecedented opportunities. Digitization and the other themes enabled by the Internet collectively bring society into a culture of speed (compression), marketing to units of one (customization), a brand new world that blends products and services (informatization), and manufacturing in lots of one (convergence).

Digitization by itself is not very useful. Only when it is combined with one of the other themes does it usually create value. For example, customization is impossible without digitization. Once customer information is digitized, it is ready for databasing, sorting, and broadcasting over the Internet. The Internet makes it possible for companies to move data from an online order form to the factory floor.

＊The biggest implication of digitization is how it enables the separation of form from function. Separation of function and form involves the delivery of a given function by different means. Digitization enables service companies to separate the functions of their services from their traditional forms or packaging, creating new markets and opportunities in the process.

If the function of the opportunity you are considering can be separated from its form, be cautious. The fundamental value proposition of the business is at risk. For example, selling CDs on the Net is a risky business now because digitization and the MP3 format make it inviting to download music (the function) without buying the disk (the form). Same thing with test equipment. Why should anyone buy a test hardware such as a heart monitor when the function

＊ Function is the intrinsic value of the item.
Form = the means by which it is exclusively delivered.

can be delivered on the Net? The lesson: make sure the value proposition of your opportunity leverages function, not form.

7. Informatization: Smart Products Are Proliferating

Call it penetrating intelligence. If you can't find a way to put "smartness" into your products, your competitor will. In the Net Economy, products are "informated." Technology is embedded in and around products in ways that facilitate a steady stream of information about transactions and the use to which products and services are put. As in the case of most network software, customers turn features on or off depending on their preferences. The product itself is a primary interface between the end user, the manufacturer, distributors, and other parties with whom the customer wants to communicate.

Products that communicate with manufacturers or infomediaries, also known as "smart products," will improve performance, reduce costs, and increase revenues. The most obvious example of the proliferation of smart products is the addition of embedded computer chips to virtually every mechanical device in our lives. Most people are aware of the role of embedded computer chips in automobiles. Today, the dollar value of a car's smart electronics is overtaking the value of its steel body. We suspect that chips inhabit electronic gear such as microwave ovens and stereos. But embedded chips also proliferate in such ubiquitous appliances as elevators, air conditioners, garage door openers, hotel door locks, ATMs, refrigerators, and soft drink machines.

Are the opportunities you are considering constantly adding intelligence to existing products or services? If not, someone else will insert themselves in your value chain and capture value that will no longer go to you.

8. Compression: Transaction Costs Are Being Slashed

Perhaps the Net Economy's most dramatic impact on commerce is its role in systematically reducing transaction costs. By steadily squeezing transaction costs out of the virtual value chain, compression will continue to transform every aspect of interacting with customers. In the traditional economy, it cost about one dollar to keep information about an individual customer. Today, it costs considerably less than one cent per customer. Lower transaction costs allow companies to control and track information that would have been too costly to capture and process just a few years ago. Any assessment of the true impact of the Net Economy must include the lower transaction costs that are unleashing network effects, increasing returns, and creating economies of scope and scale. In this way, the Net Economy is remaking the structure of companies and industries alike.

Compression and the other trends discussed in this chapter work together to squeeze out many of the traditional costs of interactions—the searching, coordinating, and monitoring that customers and companies must do when they exchange goods, services, or ideas. Compression comes in a multitude of shapes and forms. In its most powerful form, it is not even recognizable as a separate force. But whatever shape it assumes, compression squeezes out or eliminates the most costly pieces of the marketing, fulfillment, and customer service processes. The more commodity-oriented the service and support components are, the more ruthlessly compression consigns them to history.

Compression, the Net Economy trend that squeezes distance and time out of the equation, eliminates most of the costs that the traditional economy has long assumed to be more or less fixed. Compression is the force that makes distance irrelevant. Geography, the consideration that until now has played a key role in determining who competed with whom, is massively expensive. In the Net Economy, your business can connect instantly with customers all over the globe. Of course, compression enables the flipside of this benefit as well: you're exposed to worldwide competitors who have just as easy access to your customers as you have to theirs.

Take a good look at the job or initiative you are considering in terms of its cycle times and transaction costs. Rest assured that potential competitors are doing the same thing. If you can see opportunities for compression, they can, too.

9. Time Is Money: Why Speed Matters

It's all about velocity. The quicker you can move, the more advantage you have. The faster you can go, the more you can leave the competition playing catch-up. Speed reduces friction and costs. By collapsing time and breeding accelerated change, the Net Economy has succeeded in further reducing transaction costs. Successful Net Economy players accept a culture of constant change and are willing to break down and continually reconstruct their products and processes— even the most successful ones. In a world of instantaneous connection, there is a huge premium on instant response and the ability to learn from and adapt to the marketplace in real time.

Let's hope the process underlying the position you are considering has already been re-engineered to eliminate every redundancy and unnecessary operation. If not, let's hope you can suggest what can be eliminated to speed up the cycle times.

10. Advantage Is Becoming More Temporary

How does one create advantage in the Net Economy? First, let's distinguish between old and new ways of conceptualizing advantage. Throughout the industrial age, it was rational for managers to focus on achieving competitive advantage, and once having achieved it, to sustain it. When the basic building blocks of success were measured in the scarcity of raw materials, markets, capital, and labor, organizing these elements better than your competitors created value. When the economy is a zero-sum game ("if we have one more of these, you have one less"), competitive advantage is probably something worth protecting. Unfortunately, the energy and resources spent protecting advantage cannot be applied where it really counts: innovating on behalf of your customers.

As we entered the information age, our mistake was to assume that information technology (IT) by itself could drive sustainable competitive advantage. It doesn't work that way, even though some IT initiatives move companies forward and help create value. Relying on technology to generate competitive advantage is counterproductive for a number of reasons. First, it places way too much emphasis on technology at a time when technology can be quickly and easily duplicated. There's no advantage to having something that can be easily duplicated. Second, aiming toward competitive advantage misses the point. Competitive advantage should not be the goal. It should be the result of something much more basic: offering customers a product or service that saves them time, makes their lives easier, or enriches their relationships. We derive competitive advantage from doing that well.

The Net delivers magnificent rewards to its earliest adopters—stratospheric market caps, unlimited revenue streams, broad communities of customers, limitless opportunities for virtual partnerships. But don't make the mistake of thinking that the advantages are anything more than transitory. Is the leadership of the organization you are considering joining content to rest on first mover advantage? If so, give it a pass. By the time you get up to speed, the advantage will be with someone else. Who will that be? Your challenge is to find that train and get onboard.

3
Contract Work

Job security is gone. The driving force of a career
must come from the individual.

—Homa Bahrami

PERMANENT OR TEMPORARY?

You've no doubt heard about Web designers who work on a contract basis
at night so they can surf during the day and are paid at twice the rate of the
guy doing the same thing in the next cubicle who happens to be a permanent
employee.

It's true, but they don't get stock options or, for the most part, benefits.

On the other hand, if it's any consolation to you, remember this truism: All
jobs are temporary.

That's the way it is in every corner of the Net Economy. Net companies are
especially eager to embrace the benefits of being agile by looking outward to a
multitude of outsourcing solutions powered by a workforce of contingent employees. In Silicon Valley, up to 40 percent of the workforce can be considered
contingent employees. This trend is especially noticeable in the temporary help
industry where, since 1984, employment has grown at a rate nearly ten times
the overall employment growth in that region. Currently, there are more than
250 temporary help agency offices in Silicon Valley alone.

There is some evidence that substantial sectors of the American corporate
structure favor moving to a predominantly contingent workforce. Listen to
James Meadows, Vice President for Human Resources at AT&T: "People need
to look at themselves as self-employed, as vendors who come to this company to sell their skills. In AT&T, we have to promote the concept of the whole

workforce being contingent, though most of our contingent workers are inside our walls. 'Jobs' are being replaced by 'projects' and 'fields of work.'"

Wells Fargo, too, has announced that it is moving to a contingent workforce model in which only midlevel managers and up will be full-time employees of the enterprise. Everyone else will be contingent.

James R. Ziegler, executive director of Professional Association of Contract Employees (PACE), is happy with this development. He believes that free agency is the model for the future because it makes all workers responsible for themselves and their benefits. "Companies are starting to outsource all their operations and keep only middle-management people to make the strategic decisions," says Ziegler, author of the *Contract Employees Handbook*. "We're developing into a society that may be jobless but not workless," he says, adding, "My goal is to make it possible for a downsized full-time employee to enter the contingent workforce and not give up any benefits, and at the same time to have the advantages of the self-employed." The Contract Employee's Newsletter is published by the Professional Association of Contract Employees (www.pacepros.com).

In 1997 there were 14 million self-employed workers and an additional 8.3 million independent contractors. "Individuals have massive amounts of corporate power compared to what used to be," says Daniel Pink, the creator of FreeAgentNation.com (www.freeagentnation.com), a hub of information for all types of nontraditional workers. With the availability of technology, cell phones, scanners, computers, and all else, one can become as productive as many, Pink suggests. The free-agent worker illustrates the "flexibility" of the new economy. "People realized that if they're not getting security, they might as well have flexibility," Pink says. "The old arrangement found employees trading freedom for security—that bargain doesn't exist anymore. In fact, having all eggs in one basket is actually less secure."

We used to have a model of employment in the United States that envisioned a business enterprise with full-time employees and full-time employment. Many generations of people worked their entire careers with one employer. People talked of loyalty between employee and employer. Changing jobs was considered suspect and losing a job was shameful.

The Internet and the extended information revolution have disrupted the economy so completely that this model of employment is now almost quaint. The pace of change and global competition have forced large businesses to keep their core workforces to a minimum. As critical skills became more portable, the workers started to move around. Workers lives became more complex, with a variety of lifestyles that fought against the limitations of the traditional nine-to-five workweek. At the same time, companies needed to be more agile, adding and discarding resources as their business fortunes ebbed and flowed.

The result? Amazing new opportunities and entry points into the job market. Of course, there's nothing terribly new about all this. We've always had a temporary worker industry, but the contingent workforce industry, as it is now called, has gone upscale, representing not only secretarial but also technical, professional, and managerial workers. They earn salaries and benefits that reflect their higher skills. And some companies are creating their own internal "temporary" workforce, which provides greater flexibility. There are even newsletters, associations, and unions for portable workers.

What is new about the contingent workforce is the innovative ways companies are working with "just-in-time people" to get jobs done. No longer are contingent employees called upon simply to answer the phones when the secretary is on vacation. Instead, more than 80 percent of Internet companies use contingent workers as a way to respond to changes in demand for their goods and services. Alternative work arrangements give companies the flexibility they need to stay responsive in an increasingly competitive marketplace, but they also provide employees with the flexibility they need. Estimates of the size of the contingent workforce vary from 10 to 35 percent of the total workforce, depending on how it is defined.

For the purposes of this chapter, let's define contingent work as any work that does not carry the expectation by the employer or employee of regular, full-time employment. Few employers use the term *permanent* to describe full-time work because lawyers feel it establishes the basis for an employment contract. In any event, you probably have contributed to the popularity of contingent workers. If you ever held a part-time job, assistantship, internship, or co-op position, you were likely counted as among the contingent workforce.

Sometimes the argument about full-time versus contingent work takes on the attributes of a religious debate. Those who argue that temporary work is great work say that modern temporary workers are empowered individuals with the freedom to sell their work to the most attractive offer. These people point to the massive layoffs of the late 1980s and early 1990s in which white-collar workers were released from organizations at an unprecedented rate, so that, in 1990, a third of unemployed workers were estimated to come from these types of positions.

Those who conclude that temporary work is bad work argue that companies exploit temporary workers to gain flexibility in the size and skills of their workforces. The moral argument is that it turns workers into commodities. Some people lament the end of paternalism. Instead of carrying workers with once-needed but now obsolete skills on its payroll, companies can hire and release temporary workers as needed. Most often, those jobs that companies choose to fill with temporary employees are the least powerful and lowest paid. In other words, the workers most likely to be forced to accept temporary work are the ones least likely to be able to afford periods of unemployment between assignments. These disposable workers allow organizations to offer more incentives to regular workers who have skills essential to meeting customer demands and which are not readily available on the open market.

ALTERNATIVES TO FULL-TIME WORK

If you want alternatives to regular, full-time work, you have lots of opportunities. Here are just a few:

Temporary Work

This is the stuff of Manpower and the other temporary help agencies. Most employers hire temporary workers for vacation and illness substitutes, peak workloads, and staffing new enterprises. Human resource (HR) managers can and do recruit temporary workers directly through networking, advertising, or canvassing their files of applicants or retirees. But most HR managers find it convenient to hire through temporary help agencies. More than 1.5 million temps are referred daily by agencies. The company specifies the skills needed, and the temp agency refers people with those skills, which are sometimes determined by testing. Since these workers are employed by the agency, the company eliminates problems of recruiting, terminating, and preparing tax forms. Agencies that began supplying office help have expanded to provide nurses, engineers, drafters, accountants, assemblers, managers, and any type of employee that is in demand. Some companies have established internal temp agencies, using current or former employees whose jobs have been eliminated. This approach is convenient for companies that have downsized and seek to find work for laid-off employees. The arrangement also provides the company with employees who are familiar with company procedures and policies and may even return to their former jobs.

Part-Time Work

This is generally taken on by people who want but can't get full-time work. The Bureau of Labor Standards defines part-time work as anything less than thirty-five hours per week. The number of hours worked in a week involves legal issues relating to taxes, benefits, and overtime pay. Although part-time workers are contingent, their status sometimes continues over many years, as in grocery stores, restaurants, and banks. These arrangements provide financial benefits to the employer, but employees who wish to work part-time can benefit also.

Contract Employees

These are skilled temporary employees who are employed by a contract employment agency and assigned to a client company under terms specified by a contract between the agency and the client company. Contract employees are often referred to as leased employees or technical temps. Two characteristics distinguish a contract employee from other temporary employees: 1) A contract employee has specialized job skills that are usually not available within the client company, and 2) a contract employee makes lots more money. Arrangements can include a fee for a specified project or a commitment for a number of days of service. The employer does not have to deal with taxes and benefits because independent contractors are not employees. The Internal Revenue Service has strict rules for defining "independent contractors" and imposes penalties for employers who misclassify employees as independent contractors.

Let's drill down to consider two extremes of contract employees. At one end of the spectrum are agency-dependent contract employees, and at the other end are agency-independent direct consultants. All contract workers fall somewhere on this continuum. The traditional temp agency model defines the first extreme in which the contractor depends entirely upon the contract employment agency for his or her livelihood. In this model the agency locates the assignment, the agency recruits the contractor, the agency negotiates with the client, the agency bills the client, and the agency pays the contractor on payday after withholding the agency's cut of the bill as well as all applicable taxes.

As one moves away from the traditional model and progresses toward the opposite extreme, the influence of the agency is diminished. Control transfers from the agency to the contractor, and eventually the agency has no control at all. In the traditional model the contractor works for the agency. At the opposite extreme the agency works for the contractor. Just where you settle on the continuum is, after all, a personal decision that has to do with your comfort level and immediate circumstances. But most of all it has to do with your understanding of how the contracting industry operates, and how you can use that information to your best advantage. Your income and your professional security are strongly influenced by where you fall along the continuum. Ideally, all things considered, you want to progress as far from the traditional model as possible.

Consultants

These are a special class of independent contractors. Consultants consult. That is, they are paid to offer advice or to carry out a specific project with a specific deliverable. Consulting firms are outside vendors, and they may have thousands of employees, or only one. For billing purposes, the client may require a consulting firm to report aggregate hours broken out by project, but the work efforts of individual employees of the consulting firm are never tracked by the client. Independent contractors are frequently referred to correctly as consultants. Recruiting firms like to refer to themselves as consulting firms because of the role they play in helping companies locate qualified workers, but the term often stretches credulity.

Employee Leasing

This involves a company outsourcing complete human resources administration for a class of employees. Companies like Microsoft are famous (or infamous) for contracting with an employee leasing company to supply a workgroup with a programmer or analysts on a long-term basis. The team leader is the supervisor, but the agency is the employer of record and takes care of all hiring, payrolls, administrative paperwork, regulatory matters, and benefits. The same arrangement can be used for database administrators, physicians, or any other type of workforce. Leased workforces can range from one to several hundred employees.

Home-Based Work

This involves a class of assignments that employees can do at home, more or less at the times of their choosing. These tasks include word processing, accounting, programming, craft work, or assembly. The employer may or may not provide materials and does not have to provide work space. Home-based workers can choose their own hours, interrupt work for child care and other tasks, and take time out for any personal reason. They may be employed full-time on a long-term basis, but they commonly work for one employer. Home-based contingent workers are different from salaried employees who telecommute, that is, do some of their work at home by computer or telephone.

Interns

These are not "employees" under commonly understand definitions, mainly because their compensation is in the form of experience, not money. Interns participate in every aspect of a company's operations, doing tasks under supervision that paid staff does. If an intern is paid, he or she is really a co-op student or trainee.

Co-op Students

These rotate between formal classroom education and on-the-job experiences. Students in cooperative education programs that alternate work and study can be an important source of contingent workers. More than 200,000 students from more then 1,000 colleges and universities participate in programs that combine classroom instruction with periods of work, usually paid.

CAREERS IN THE CONTINGENT WORKFORCE

If you are going to consider a stint as a temporary worker, you need to decide if you are going to go independent or be represented. There are advantages to both decisions. It's okay to be a traditional temporary employee. Millions of workers prefer this arrangement. The traditional model is designed after the classic temporary employment agency. Employers routinely hire temps to perform Web maintenance or coding, or to fill in when E-commerce peakloads go up (around Christmas). What distinguishes the contract employee from other temps is this: Contract employees provide specific, advanced, technical, and professional skills. Contract employees are paid more than regular temps, and they tend to have longer assignments. However, in every other respect contract employees are just like regular temps, and traditional contract employment agencies operate just like regular temporary employment agencies—but other contractors prefer, or are forced, to be represented by agencies.

Why would you want to be represented and give a chunk of the value you create to an agency? Sometimes you might not have a choice. A number of enterprises have policies that prevent them from dealing with independent contractors. If you think about it, it makes sense. Some of these companies engage thousands of contractors. It would be an administrative nightmare for them to have thousands of different agreements. For that reason, they prefer to deal with temporary staffing agencies, which can provide the bodies and keep the paperwork simpler.

The Net Economy will continue to favor contract employees. The question for you is how to protect yourself and optimize your opportunities. The Net Economy is spawning new types of representation for contract workers, including full-service and pass-through agencies and a number of variants. Full details on the features, limitations, and benefits of each of these models are provided at the *Internet Jobs!* Web site. Also available is the full text of the *Contract Employers Handbook.* I am especially indebted to its author, James Ziegler, Ph.D., for permitting me to include on the Web site the Contractor's Bill of Rights, a manifesto Dr. Ziegler believes all organizations employing contingent workers ought to honor.

PART 2
Internet Jobs

Solving a problem simply means representing it so as to make the solution transparent.

—Herbert Simon, The Sciences of the Artificial

It's all about people. It's all about jobs.

For all its emphasis on technology and networking, the Net Economy depends on intellectual capital. Without people like you who have a deep familiarity with the underpinnings of the Internet and are willing to apply it in a job, it would collapse in no time.

You have the skills. There is a demand for those skills. In fact, there is a greater number of jobs chasing a smaller number of skills. The challenge is to put the skills and jobs together. Fortunately, the Net itself makes the process of matching employees and employers more empowering and manageable than ever before. Still, not every applicant gets the outcomes he or she wants or even deserves. Why not? Because employers have their own agendas. Here are four lessons that might give struggling job seekers a better understanding of why employers behave the way they do.

- The skills shortage is not the same in every area of IT.
- A company may be desperate for workers and at the same time turn down applicants who are almost—but not quite—qualified.
- Employers will take experience over education every time.
- You need to know what your background says about you and your work to counter any negative impressions.

Part II of *Internet Jobs!* looks at the three major types of careers available in the Net Economy, along with what skills you'll need, what employers are looking for, and what the jobs entail. Chapter 4 describes the jobs that develop and manage the content side of the Net Economy. Chapter 5 describes the jobs that focus on the infrastructure of the Net Economy. We have noted that Net businesses are businesses first, and they must be run as such. Chapter 6 lists many of the business jobs that are most essential to the success of any Net initiative. You've never heard of some of the most exciting jobs created by the Net Economy. Chapter 7 describes some emerging job categories for you to consider.

4
Content Jobs

Every morning I get up and look through the Forbes list of the richest people in America. If I'm not there, I got to work.

—Robert Orben, American Humorist

CONTENT ASCENDANT

The Net will always need content providers, for without content the Net is an empty shell. Because editorial or graphical talent is necessary, however, it is not sufficient for success on the Net. To make it in the Net Economy, think of the unique attributes that the Net imposes on everything it touches: interactivity, multimedia, digitization, and personalization. If you can be creative, and preferably outrageous, while seamlessly including these elements, you have a shot at success in the content end of the Net Economy, the only part of the Net Economy with a real future.

At this point in the evolution of the Internet, content takes a decided back seat to infrastructure. Content is boring. Infrastructure is sexy. That's the way it is—but not for long. The inexorable logic of the Internet will soon reverse this condition, and people who plan a career in the content end of the Net Economy will be rewarded. Here's why. In the Net Economy, technological advantage simply cannot be sustained. The relentless pace of the Internet quickly commoditizes all technology. No matter how exciting and magical when it is first created, all technology eventually devolves into a commodity, and the Net Economy demonstrates that the value of commodities eventually approaches zero. Your work building infrastructure, no matter how inspired, will quickly become generic and unremarkable.

Content, simply put, will not suffer from that particular dynamic. In the digital world, great technology can (and will) be duplicated. Great content providers such as yourself cannot be duplicated. Many organizations that have mature infrastructures have already figured this out. America Online is busy acquiring content. Sony and Yahoo! are spending big bucks buying media companies or creating original content. Other Web companies, such as Internet service providers, will start doing the same as soon as they realize their businesses have become commodities.

Content will emerge as the only way to increase the appeal of a Web site to attract eyeballs and create "stickiness," the inestimable quality of a Web site that attracts consumers, and entices them to pay attention and ideally part with some cash. The online auction site, eBay (www.ebay.com), is one such site. Most portal sites have their strategies directed at keeping traffic within their domains, hence the large number of partnerships among sites. The Net Economy increasingly looks to content professionals to create the direct sensory experience that makes Web sites stand out. When that happens, look for huge shifts in valuation as the market starts to reward the message more than the medium.

THE CONVERGENCE OF CONTENT CAREERS

Convergence in the Net Economy describes the phenomenon of two or more existing forces, technologies, markets, producers, or boundaries combining to create a new force that is more powerful and more efficient than the sum of its parts. Convergence is not a new dynamic; it has been going on as long as human beings have been developing and refining technologies, roles, and markets. In this case, the skills required of content providers and the tools they use will converge with the skills and tools used by developers and other technical professionals. In a complete vindication of Marshall MacLuhan's observation that "the medium is the message," Web content providers make the infrastructure and technology as much a part of the message as the editorial and graphic work they create. The consumers of the Net Economy are indistinguishable from the providers. It is no longer possible for content people to leave the technology to "them." There is no "them" anymore. There's only more of "us."

Just as raw data has little real value, raw content is uninteresting. First of all, there's just so much of it. Most content today is devoid of the context to make it meaningful. To make it in the Net Economy, think of the unique attributes that the Net imposes on everything it touches: interactivity, multimedia, digitization, and personalization. Mix those elements of editorial content and media together in compelling new ways to create context and community. If you want to succeed as a content provider, your art and media skills will have to be integrated with meta-content strategies. Meta-content is content about content. A page of thumbnail images, each of which is clickable, is meta-content. It organizes content and makes the images more manageable and accessible. A meta-content approach to the task brings to bear all the multidisciplinary skills you have at your command: human factors, semiotics, psychology, cognitive science, and information management.

MULTIMEDIA GRAPHIC SKILLS

The Net supports many types of media. Today, a large chunk of the Net is basically brochureware: material from the world of print dumped onto the Web. Brochureware is static and two-dimensional. We need to move away from just fixed media, that is anything that is created, saved, stored, and delivered exactly the same way over and over. Fixed media constitutes all print and most television and radio. There is nothing wrong with fixed media per se, but for the Web it is flat and lifeless. What the Web needs is dynamic or interactive media. Examples of this genre can be found in many CD-ROMs, interactive TV, computer gaming, and the Internet. In an interactive medium, exquisite personalization is possible, resulting in markets of one in which each consumer is served a unique message. The audience gets to shape the experience by their choices. The commitment to inform a particular message by the choices and interests of each consumer places a heavy burden on the shoulders of those who do the original project design, storyboarding, and event sequencing.

MULTIMEDIA GRAPHIC COMPETENCIES REQUIRED

If you want a Net position as a content provider, here are just some of the competencies and minimal skills you'll need to demonstrate:

- **Animating** in either animated GIF images or Java for most Web sites.
- **Adjusting** gamma values and calibrating drawing programs and systems to account for color variations
- **Applying** special effects to graphics
- **Compositing and Layout** involve the creating and arranging of visual elements and the organization of relationship. Net design demands the cleanest and highest levels of organization. Skill sets require familiarity with desktop publishing, most notably Quark's Xpress. For Web layout, employers will expect experience with Microsoft's FrontPage, DeltaPoint's QuickSite, and Adobe Systems' PageMill.
- **Computer Aided Design** (CAD) assisting in the design and drawing of 2-D and 3-D models of objects. AutoDesk's AutoCAD is the industry standard. The Net Economy requires experience with using CAD programs to create wireframes that can be converted to VRML (Virtual Reality Modeling Language) for use on the Web.
- **Converting** graphics formats and adjusting associated color schemes. The good news is that the Web is getting away from its text origins and getting

more graphical. The bad news is that professionals who create and manipulate the graphics need to be up on at least four standards:

1. **Bitmapped graphic files** (sometimes called "raster" graphics) associates points on an image with color values for each specific point. Bitmapped graphics are made with paint programs or created via a scanner. The standard bitmapped formats are the GIF and JPEG.

2. **Indexed color** (sometimes called "mapped" color) allows for high-quality Web images of the smallest possible size.

3. **RGB color** uses independent values of red, green, and blue to construct all other colors.

4. **Vector images** (also known as object-oriented images) are constructed of mathematically described elements by using drawing programs. Vector images are the graphics format of choice when an image will be resized by the user.

- **Dithering** reduces the number of colors in an indexed color image and compensating for the colors that were removed by approximation.

- **Event Sequencing** is the simulation of time by controlling movement through events. It is an integral part of animation and most interactive media. Some disciplines include clickstream development, a series of mouse-clicks through a Web site, forward kinematics, a technique used to make 3-D actions more lifelike, and adaptive presentation, an automated storyboarding and path-planning technique.

- **Image Processing and Conversion** require a subtle mix of skills. The Net's many constraints—architectures, standards, protocols, platforms, operating systems, and output devices—impose considerable difficulties on designers. The standard tool in this area is Adobe's PhotoShop. Employers demand familiarity with the following skill sets: vector images, bitmapped or raster graphic files, index or mapped color, RGB color.

- **Iconography** is widely used by the Net to communicate in place of words. It's ironic that before literacy was common, icons were widely used, and now that literacy is widespread, icons are more important than ever. On the Net, icons are important for two main reasons. First, people don't have time to read. Second, globalism means that you can't assume everyone will speak your language. Well-considered icons solve both problems. A study of semiotics, the science of a culture's unspoken symbols, may be useful.

- **Illustration and Drawing** remain essential skills. Even in the Net Economy, it is useful to create images on a drawing board. The Net prizes the ability to convert abstractions into immediately meaningful images differentiated by the use of line, shapes, shading, and forms. Nevertheless, most creation is done via the use of clipart and graphic primitives for 3-D worlds.

- **Interactivity** includes CD-ROMs, interactive TV, and computer gaming.

- **Lighting and Perspective** competencies allow producers of content for the Net present to better communicate their ideas.

- **Manipulating** colormaps, including dithering, helps to reduce color debt and consolidate colormaps.

- **Scanning** and sizing images

- **Sound and music** are extremely sophisticated in today's multimedia Web sites. Voice-recognition software will make sound increasingly important. Working knowledge of the MIDI format and other emerging standards is critical.

- **Static images** are of critical importance in all e-commerce Web sites, requiring working expertise of GIF, JPEG, and other graphic standards.

- **Three-Dimensional Environments** (3-D graphical interfaces) are just beginning to emerge (e.g., The Real World 3-D Interface option of CA's Unicenter TNG) but are still not quite mainstream.

- **Video** skills are imperative as bandwidth increases, making streaming video, MPEG, and other technologies more popular.

- **Virtual Reality Modeling Language** (VRML) is poised to become the core technology for creating virtual environments in more than two dimensions.

- **Typography,** new fonts, and other typographical elements are requirements of the Net. As the Web emerges as a standard, fonts uniquely tailored to the Web will have to emerge. Font portability between hardware platforms is critical.

MULTIMEDIA SPECIALTIES

Because multimedia is a new concept, traditional employers are still in the process of formulating their needs. As a result, many multimedia developers are self-employed, and they frequently work on a freelance basis. The nature of this employment situation provides an opportunity to work on a variety of projects, such as designing a Web site, authoring a commercial CD-ROM title, creating an interactive promotional demo, building a user-interface prototype, integrating networking technology into an interactive kiosk, or animating an educational presentation.

Information alone won't cut it. You have to make someone want to read it. Whether creating for the Web, a training video, or the latest computer game, compelling presentation is key in getting your company's message across.

As a multimedia specialist, you are given an idea to bring to life. You determine the best tools and format to use for your presentation. Before you jump in, you estimate how long the job will take and determine whether to call in additional help from inside or outside your company. The size of the project and budget often determine this for you. When designing, you set the tone and pace, select colors, and create a visually appealing layout.

The tools you use change at an incredible pace, so you stay informed about upcoming products and tools that can make your job easier or enhance the presentation of the material. In a world driven by moving images, you strive to offer something new and exciting to capture the attention of your company's target audience. Specialties in multimedia development include the following content producers.

Multimedia Director

A multimedia developer works with today's newest advances in desktop computer technology. A developer draws on the skills of the computer programmer and the visual artist to integrate graphics, text, and digital audio and video with interactivity. This multimedia content can be delivered on CD-ROM, over the World Wide Web, or even on floppy disk.

Multimedia developers are critical to satisfy the insatiable demand for rich content by Net consumers. At the broadest level, the work of multimedia developers is the generation and manipulation of graphic images, animations, sound, text, and video into consolidated and seamless multimedia programs. Multimedia applications are as diverse as their component technologies; they include Web sites and pages, computer-based interactive training, data presentation and information kiosks, CD-ROMs, entertainment and educational products, and multimedia presentations. Multimedia developers generally undertake the following tasks:

- Investigating, analyzing, and recommending appropriate platforms and software to achieve the client's objectives
- Preparing flow diagrams and storyboards outlining the product concept and treatment
- Preparing code to produce the multimedia product
- Preparing in digital format 2- and 3-dimensional graphic images, animations, video/sound production and editing, scanning photographs and images, retouching and manipulating
- Preparing instructional-design and screen-design concepts
- Consulting with related graphics, production, and engineering experts
- Project managing the development and implementation of multimedia products.

Requirements of Multimedia Directors
- High-order technical skills
- Ability to visualize and conceptualize

- Creativity, imagination, and artistic flair
- Effective team leadership and team membership
- Client focus
- Commitment to understanding and utilizing new technology
- High-order project management skills and ability to work to deadlines
- Ability to direct the work of others
- High degree of drawing skill and feeling for movement and timing
- Sense of color, space, and form
- Patience and attention to detail

Artist/Graphics Designer

Net artwork is now a popular component of personal Web pages, commercial Web sites, online magazines, and online galleries. Due to the increase in Web usage for commercial advertising and publishing, there has been a large increase in the need for people with art and graphics skills to aid in producing eye-catching art for advertising. The objective is to incorporate enough graphics to attract a reader's attention.

The artist/graphics designer is generally responsible for Web page layout and design of magazines, newspapers, journals, and other publications. Since multimedia on the Web has become more prevalent, artist/graphics designers also create graphics for computer-generated media. These persons either create HTML pages or communicate with the Web page designer to produce quality artwork that properly represents the textual information. The skills necessary to do this are graphics design and creativity. The artist should have a working knowledge of the popular paint and scan programs, such as Adobe Photoshop, and experience with some desktop publishing package. Another name for the occupation is *visual artist*. The demand for art/graphics designers is frequently for a freelance or consultant position. Magazines and commercial businesses will hire persons to perform graphics design on a regular basis, given that they have other skills to complement their design ability.

Computer-Based Graphic Designer

Computing technology and specialist software packages are used to manage the production, interface, and integration of various graphics and other mediums into the multimedia package design. The graphic designer's primary role in the multimedia context is the design of art and copy layouts for CD-ROM and multimedia products. It is possible to specialize further and focus on particular industry sectors, such as advertising, corporate design, Internet applications, or exhibition design.

Instructional Design

The design and development of content and curriculum products, learning-support resources, and delivery/assessment methodologies has applications in contexts such as teaching, learning, and information distribution. Instructional designers increasingly use the flexibility offered by multimedia applications to target specific learning objectives and particular audiences. The incorporation of multimedia technologies in instructional design work can provide a combination of interactivity, the management features of computer-based training, plus the benefits of realistic audio and video.

Multimedia Developers

The system and applications programming issues around conversion between platforms (for example CDi, Mac) entail the initial writing of code for incorporation of text, graphics, video, animation, digital/analog photographs, audio, and 2- or 3-D modeling. Within this specialty, further specializations are possible, for example video systems development programming and PC lead programming. Multimedia programming could also be considered as a subset of applications programming

Author-Based Developers

These developers apply appropriate multimedia authoring technologies to conceptualize, design, assemble, and integrate a variety of images, text, animation, and sound before selecting and applying the desired program structure to produce a multimedia end-product. In a programming sense, this may involve writing scripts, using namespaces and packages, and writing extensions. The term *authoring a multimedia sequence* is sometimes used in this context.

Digital Video-Sound Editors

These editors are involved with the computer-based editing of video sound for multimedia products. Working under instruction from directors, editors make editorial decisions with regard to the mood, pace, and climax of sound effects. This involves working closely with other professional staff to analyze, evaluate, and select sound effects for integration with images and other mediums.

Animators

The design, drawing, layout, and production of animation sequences incorporated in multimedia products are the duties of the animator. Traditionally, they have worked in film and television, but multimedia provides a new and challenging extension for creative animators. Animators may participate in the production of storyboards and stop-motion animation (flat plane, modeling), as well as drawing cartoon and other characters in a succession of related movements to create an illusion of movement. Some further specialization is possible, for example as a 3-D graphic animator.

Multimedia Competencies Required

- Personal Computer Basics
- Internet Basics
- Microsoft Office
- Windows 95 or Windows 98
- Multimedia Training
- Art Theory and Principles of Design
- Graphic Design
- Typography
- Animation
- Graphic Design Software Programs
- Web Site Design Skills

MULTIMEDIA EDITORIAL ROLES

For all the talk that the Net is driven by graphics, the written (and perhaps spoken) word will remain the critical determinant of success. That means that written communication is and will continue to be perhaps the core competency in the Net Economy. That does not mean written communication in English only. Competencies in other languages, especially Japanese, Chinese, and other Asian languages, will be very much in demand.

Advertising and Marketing

E-commerce is booming. It represents a new world of opportunities for sales, advertising, and marketing professionals. What will it take for you to enter the management levels of e-commerce and develop the advertising and marketing programs that will dominate the future of virtual sales? Are you interested in corporate Web sites that project an organization's image and advertises a company's products and services, or are you interested in direct sales of products such as books, software, and CDs?

Animator

Why is there no Web-based equivalent of Mickey Mouse or even Dilbert or Peanuts? The popularity of animation on the Web has been hampered by a number of factors: lack of standards, bandwidth issues, cost considerations, and lack of talent. Nevertheless, the most progressive organizations acknowledge that animation can be a powerful way to communicate a message.

Illustrator

The Net prizes the ability to convert abstractions into immediately meaningful images differentiated by the use of line, shapes, shading, and forms. While the native ability to draw is still useful, most creation on the Web is done via the use of clipart and graphic primitives for 3-D worlds.

Photographer

Digital photography is the medium of content providers on the Net. Skill in manipulating the hardware and, more importantly, software such as PhotoShop, are mandatory.

Producer

With the proliferation of new media, people responsible for specific types of content are called "producers" or "content providers." For example, there are sound producers, CD-ROM producers, and video producers. The term *producer* may also describe people who integrate various modes of media into a more complex whole. Increasingly, producers are called on to manage the complete life-cycle of editorial objects (images, data, text, video, animation, etc.).

Translator

As the Web becomes increasingly global, English will no longer be the dominant language. In such an environment, it is no surprise that the demand for capable language translators is growing. It can go two ways. The Net may make human translators indispensable. Here's a scenario: Just before an executive in Tokyo takes an important meeting, he switches on a pocket device that electronically sends out a request for a translator. He specifies his requirements. Language? Japanese. Duration of meeting? Thirty minutes. Fee? One hundred dollars per minute. His request is instantly bid out, brokered, and selected. Moments later, the executive is connected and ready to go. Sounds great, right? But there's a fly in the ointment. Translation software is getting better all the time. There's an even chance that most of the translation the Net requires will be handled automatically, without human intervention.

Writer

The Net Economy demands a new kind of writing. Just as writing for a TV script requires a different set of writer's muscles than writing for, say, a magazine, writing a Web-enabled brochure is radically different from writing a print brochure. We believe that while good Net writing can be learned, it cannot be taught. The mechanics of writing can be studied, and that's important. But the kind of creative wordsmithing that the Net demands requires an attitude and lack of self-consciousness that we believe must be natural. Like obscenity, people know great writing when they see it. Employers will continue to look for candidates who have the spark of good writing in them. Frequently these candidates have in their backgrounds a broad liberal arts education reinforced by a portfolio of writing samples from the print, broadcast, and cyber worlds.

Editorial Competencies Required

To contribute high-quality editorial product for use in the Net Economy, you must demonstrate competencies in the creation and manipulation of the following competencies:

- **Metaphor,** simile, and other comparisons and analogies for communicating context and attitude
- **Chunking,** or organizing a message into bite-sized increments, to aid communication.
- **Rhyme,** rhythm, and the jargon of popular culture
- **Humor,** puns, satire, sarcasm, detachment, and irony, usually applied with a post modern, self-conscious 'tude.
- **Mimetic** triggers to enhance the effect of a message

While there may be fewer jobs in the Net Economy, there are more and more tasks. These tasks require people to take on roles. In turn, these roles create opportunities. In the following chapters, we will discuss the opportunities available right now, those that are emerging, and those whose best days are behind them.

5
Infrastructure Jobs

The art of progress is to preserve order amid change and
to preserve change amid order.

—Alfred North Whitehead

WHAT'S IN A TITLE?

Some of the most rewarding Net jobs are focused on building and maintaining the infrastructure or "plumbing" of the Internet and its applications. There is no substitute for this work, and the skills needed for these disciplines are going to be in demand for the foreseeable future. There is currently more demand for these positions than people available to fill them. When demand outstrips what you can supply, you are in the driver's seat when it comes to negotiations. If your skills are good, you can pretty much choose where you want to work.

Here we describe some of the entry-level positions for information technology (IT) professionals seeking employment in the Internet world. These positions are generally for computer science majors who want to build and maintain the infrastructure for Web sites. The work requires a wide range of experience and sometimes includes building links from the latest Java programs running on powerful Sun Microsystems workstations to legacy COBOL applications running on old IBM mainframes. Where would you fit in if you went to work in an IT department responsible for building and maintaining a corporate Web site? In each case, the chapter describes the job, includes a typical job description, lists of skills required, and the types of personal attributes companies are seeking.

There are millions of positions opening up in the Net Economy. How are we to describe them all? Fortunately, most of the jobs are subsets of established descriptions, job titles, or disciplines. Here are a few that you'll see over and over again and a few we hope will soon go the way of eight-track tapes. For example, *manager* and *administrative assistant* are old-school titles. If you see anything with the words *FORTRAN* or *COBOL,* you'll know that you're in one of the older neighborhoods of the industry. In the Net Economy, there's a whole new class of job titles coming to an e-commerce site near you. Here are some of the most common infrastructure jobs that will be in demand in the twenty-first century.

Rigid job titles and career ladders are hallmarks of an economy that valued structure and hierarchy. The industrial organization was driven by an authoritarian command-control mentality. The Net is inherently democratic. Its structure reflects flatness, not hierarchy; sharing and broad responsibility, not hoarding and tunnel vision. In some cases, there simply are no fixed job titles and job descriptions, and if there are, the job titles are fanciful, such as "Master of Chaos," or "Chief Destruction Officer."

Note: Some of the jobs described in this chapter are not, strictly speaking, Net jobs. In some cases, these jobs support the infrastructure that makes the Web possible. As such, they are not only indispensable but often are launching posts for more specific Net jobs.

HARDWARE DEVELOPMENT SKILLS

Hardware development may be facing the most significant changes in its short but momentous history. Given that the influence of hardware is decreasing relative to the role of software in business, most of the action in new Internet jobs will be software-related. As hardware becomes increasingly commodity-like, organizations put less and less emphasis on using hardware to gain competitive advantage. When companies had to put big capital investments into their mainframe computers, they had an army of hardware technicians and engineers seeing to the investment. But as hardware prices get lower and lower, the number of people dedicated to the hardware end of the Internet continues to decline. Currently there are more hardware-type workers than there are jobs available for them. As hardware prices continue their inevitable downward slope, the number of opportunities for hardware engineers and technicians will likewise diminish. Nevertheless, hardware will never go away, and the need for a certain level of hardware support skills can be projected for the near-term future.

Hardware Support

In the beginning of the industry, every hardware platform had to have an army of technicians responsible for its care and feeding. Every hardware platform had a proprietary architecture, operating system, and database file structure. The investments in hardware were staggering. Moreover, these hardware platforms had to be amortized over many years, sometimes decades. That result? Entire careers were focused on just one class of machine.

The personal computer changed all that. Customers rejected the islands of automation that came with incompatible hardware platforms. Customers rebelled at the expense of upgrading to new models every year and the difficulty of porting data from one system to another. Customers demanded openness and transparency. The PC revolution allowed hardware to become interchangeable, driving down prices and transferring many of the responsibilities of hardware technicians to the end users themselves. At a time when PCs and Macs can run the same software, few companies maintain a separate hardware support staff. All computer support people, especially end users, must have some basic hardware support skills. Such skills do not represent a growth area in the Net Economy.

Hardware Support Competencies Required

- Configure addressing on hardware
- Installing PC cards, chips, cabling
- Isolating common hardware problems
- Resolving addressing conflicts
- Setting date and time
- Setting interrupts
- Setting network parameters
- Specifying system configuration requirements
- Testing systems configurations
- Troubleshooting new problems

SOFTWARE

Today, the action on the Net is in the software domain. For better or for worse, software has become the arena in which most companies attempt to create competitive advantage. More application software is written to run on operating systems software than on hardware platforms. Establishing a brand is more and more the responsibility of software developers. The increasing complexity of software has created the need for developers who are highly skilled in one or more specialized operating systems, languages, or protocols, such as Windows NT, C++, Java, or Powerbuilder. The same complexity also breeds the need for people who can integrate all that complexity and weave them into a synergistic whole.

Operating System Support

The operating system (OS) is at the very heart of every business application. If you have good skills working with the internals of the hottest operating systems, you can write your own ticket. The trouble is knowing which OS will emerge. Lots of people bet their careers on IBM's OS2 and lost.

Most evidence points to a consolidation of operating systems. Businesses do not want the complexity of supporting multiple operating systems. These days, the smart money believes that Unix and Windows NT will emerge as the de facto operating systems in the business environment. If you obtain certification in Unix or Windows NT, you will find your skills in great demand throughout the world. Consult the *Internet Jobs!* Web site for links to certification programs. A gutsy play right now would be to focus your career on Linux, an open source variant of Unix that is making a big splash. Whether organizations will make big bets on Linux, an OS that is free but has no single owner, remains to be seen. The major operating systems supporting Net applications are:

- Windows
- Unix
- Linux
- Macintosh

Operating System Support Competencies Required

- Add peripheral software devices
- Architect infrastructure for client systems
- Asset management
- Benchmark performance against standards
- Configure network access on client system
- Configure system software
- Install systems software
- Install network access on client systems
- Manage backup and recovery
- Manage disk file-system usage
- Manage file-granting authorities
- Measure performance against service-level objectives
- Plan capacity requirements
- Resolve software device contention
- Specify archiving
- Test setup and troubleshoot novel problems

Systems Software Support

With the complexity of enterprise-wide computing come increasing demands in such areas as data security, capacity planning, asset management, performance measurement, and storage management. A class of systems software has emerged to serve this need. The growth of the Net will create upward pressure on many organizations to beef up their systems support areas. Many of the organizations will find that the cost of managing all their systems software cannot be sustained. That will create pressure to go to integrated systems software solutions such as Unicenter TNG from Computer Associates International, Hewlett-Packard's OpenView, or IBM/Tivoli's TME. Each of these systems provides a common infrastructure for managing all of an enterprise's systems software needs. Unicenter TNG appears to have the momentum in this hotly contested arena of information technology. Specific concentrations for enterprise systems software management exist in these domains:

- Backup and recovery

- Software distribution

- Network management

- Performance management

- Capacity planning

- Security

Application Software Support

Riding on top of the operating system are millions of application software packages that you can buy off the shelf. This is the software that most people actually use: word processing, desktop publishing, spreadsheets, databases. But most application software is custom-built. Securities trading systems, such as E*Trade, or online auction systems, such as eBay, have developed their equity on top of their application software. The application software is really their corporate jewel, their most prized piece of intellectual property. Without it, they have nothing. So it makes sense that they want to protect it and maintain a core competency of people who can enhance and maintain it. There isn't a variant of human activity, personal or business, which does not have application software written for it. You will be expected to have at least working knowledge of most, if not all, major applications in your company's portfolio. Fortunately, most companies have standardized on a small number of options. Further consolidation will likely result in one dominant player in each space. The top players in each category include:

- Accounting

    Peachtree Accounting

    Intuit

- Desktop publishing

    Adobe Framemaker

    Quark Xpress

- Enterprise resource planning

    SAP

    Oracle

- Graphics

    Freelance Graphics

    Harvard Graphics

- Groupware
    Lotus Notes
- Presentation
    Microsoft PowerPoint
- Personal information management
    Microsoft Outlook
    Lotus Organizer
- Project management
    Microsoft Project
    Symantec TimeLine

- Spreadsheet
    Microsoft Excel
    Lotus 1–2–3
- Web browsers
    Microsoft Explorer
    Netscape (AOL) Navigator
- Word processing
    Microsoft Word
    Corel Wordperfect

KILLER APPLICATIONS

It turns out that before any computer platform can take off commercially, it must first spawn a killer application. The PC was just a toy for hobbyists until Mitch Kapor developed the first spreadsheet. Suddenly, business people saw the value of PCs, and business was never the same again. Communications software and modems were not very interesting until e-mail came along. That got people into the swing of networking, of which the Internet is just an extension. Moreover, the Internet was a tool for scientists, virtually ignored by commercial interests until the development of the World Wide Web, which, along with e-mail, emerged as the killer app of the Internet.

E-mail continues to be the dominant service on the Net and represents a variety of career opportunities. The complexities, vagaries, and vulnerabilities of corporate e-mail will continue to demand the attention of highly compensated technicians. E-mail is now morphing into messaging systems, such as Lotus Notes and Microsoft Exchange. These systems do more than route e-mail. They serve as complete life-cycle management for messages and can also manage the entire workflow associated with forms processing. The e-mail market share is divided among systems such as:

- Lotus cc:Mail
- Microsoft Mail
- Eurdora as the client for Internet mail

To support the increasingly mission-critical network of e-mail systems, you will need familiarity with the three main e-mail application protocols:

- Single Mail Transfer Protocol (SMTP)
- Post Office Protocol (POP3)
- Internet Message Access Protocol (IMAP)

Development and Support

It is still useful to distinguish software efforts between development and support. Each demands separate skills sets. The development environment requires a high level of proficiency and attention to detail. Despite the best efforts of many organizations to impose order on the development process through the imposition of engineering disciplines, programming is in many ways still an art form. Most companies now accept this fact and make complete allowances for the idiosyncrasies of the people best suited to these tasks. Companies that tried to impose organization on their developers through the use of structured programming techniques or other methods rarely got good results. As a result, the current trend, especially among Net companies, is to free up the development environment. Although developers still have standards to maintain, and the company's business case is much better understood, it's safe to say that if you can program well, you can pretty much find the working environment you want.

PROGRAMMERS

By simplest definition, computer programmers write computer code; that is, they write the detailed instructions (programs) that tell the computer what to do to perform a certain function. Programmers write programs according to the specifications determined by systems analysts. Most programmers, regardless of whether they are writing for the Web or not, go through a similar process:

Coding: After the design process is complete, it is the job of the programmer to convert that design into step-by-step instructions according to the particular programming language in use. Coding is a precise process; even small errors in coding (widely known as "bugs") can create big problems when the program is compiled and run.

Compiling: In the case of most computer languages, before the program can be run, it must be compiled. A compiler is the computer program that converts high-level code (such as C or COBOL) into code the computer can use (binary). If the code contains severe (or fatal) errors, the program will fail to compile, and the compiler will spit out an error report telling the programmer where the errors are in the program.

Debugging: The programmer must find and correct all the errors in the code so that the program can be compiled and run.

Testing: Once the program is sufficiently error-free to compile, the programmer can then run the program with test data. Through this process, the programmer will find other errors to correct (further debugging ensues).

Maintenance: Even after a program is clean enough to release to the public, bugs and other problems may crop up. Programmers fix these problems throughout the life of the program, often resulting in updated releases of the program to registered users.

Today, most programmers use visual environments (Visual BASIC or Visual C++) plus a number of object-oriented techniques to automate much of the coding process. And programmers often do more than code. The job of programmer has come to include the kind of problem solving formerly done by systems analysts.

PROGRAMMING SPECIALTIES

Not only do programmers do more than write code, they also write code for a number of special functions.

Application (or Development) Programmers

Write original programs which allow the computer to perform certain functions. Typical applications for personal computers are spreadsheet, word processing, and game programs. Applications programmers write code for all types of systems, from PCs to mainframes, and covering all user environments, from the home to business and industry. Different programming languages are used, depending on the purpose of the program. Note: Java and C/C++ are the hot programming languages right now, widely used for scientific, business, and PC (microcomputers) applications. Traditional languages such as Fortran and Pascal are almost irrelevant. COBOL skills may be useful, but they will relegate you to maintaining legacy systems built before you were born.

Systems Programmers

Create computer operating systems (rather than applications). Systems programming requires extensive knowledge of computer architecture (specific to the particular computer under design), and is more technically demanding than general programming.

Maintenance Programmers

Adapt, customize, or "fix" large programs (for instance, large commercial applications such as payroll or inventory control) that were written by other programmers. These programmers often work in the data processing departments of large organizations such as banks or insurance companies.

Language-Specific Programmers

Specialize in one of the hundreds of computer languages, particularly those less commonly used.

Function-Specific Programmers

Specialize in one kind of application; for instance, database, network, or security systems.

OBJECT-ORIENTED PROGRAMMERS

Perhaps the hottest of today's skills, object-oriented programming will be in ferocious demand to create the database-driven Internet applications that are required to move business to the Net. To get these jobs, you will need heavy-duty skills with object languages, the most popular of which are Java and C++. Rapidly fading from interest is Smalltalk, the original object language. The good news is that these skills are in such demand that few employers have the luxury of insisting on job experience. If you can demonstrate that you can code in Java or C++ (and you'll be expected to demonstrate competence), you're in.

Java

Java is the object language most in demand. That's partly because of the support Java has received from Sun Microsystems, the move toward browser-based interfaces, and the relatively low learning curve required to master it. In many ways, Java is an outgrowth of C++. Someone with C++ skills can generally master Java in just a few weeks. From scratch, it takes a little longer, but lots of programmers have learned Java by downloading the Java Development Kit from Sun and buying a book, such as *Java in a Nutshell*.

C++

The opportunities to use C++ skills are increasing as the business world moves to an e-commerce model. Most mission-critical Web sites prefer C++ as the glue that holds everything together because of its high performance and ease of maintenance.

Smalltalk

The oldest of the object languages, it is losing ground to its offspring. Although early adopters of the Web still use Smalltalk, hiring demand for new applications has dropped considerably. You can probably still leverage your Smalltalk skills for a few more years, but you should be working on transferring your skillset to either Java or C++. The transition won't be too difficult.

It's good to know languages, but the most desirable object-oriented programmers have skills that demonstrate an awareness of how these languages can be used to solve real-world business problems. Companies want to see evidence that you can use your programming, database design and analysis, and client/server skills to design applications that handle high-volume, browser-based e-commerce transactions.

SOFTWARE ENGINEER

As a software engineer, you are involved from the beginning of the project. You look at the problem, determine the best way to address it, make a cost-benefit analysis, document your plan, and present it to management.

You gather data to identify customer requirements, resource constraints, interdependencies, and risks. You secure needed resources and coordinate your team's efforts. You select design tools, choose from architecture alternatives, and develop and validate prototypes. You lead your team in developing detailed design specifications and in writing and documenting programming code.

After you and your team have designed the software, you create a testing plan to put the application through its paces and test your product in real-world situations before going live. The challenge of being the "conductor" can be great, but so are the rewards.

The Bureau of Labor Statistics' *1998–99 Occupational Outlook Handbook* projects computing professional employment will increase by 36 percent or more through 2006—much faster than average. The Microsoft Skills 2000 July 1998 Skills Gap Survey of Microsoft solution providers and corporate customers projected 240,000 new programming hires over the next twelve months.

TECHNICAL SUPPORT SPECIALISTS

Technical support specialists are troubleshooters, providing help to their organization's computers users. Because nontechnical employees are usually not computing experts, they often run into computer problems they are unable to solve. To solve such problems, they turn to their company's technical support staff.

Specifically, technical support specialists:

- Answer phone calls from users in order to resolve specific problems
- Use automated diagnostic programs to solve problems
- Write training manuals and train users in the proper use of hardware and software
- Identify recurring problems and help users resolve them
- Oversee the daily performance of their company's computer systems
- Evaluate software programs
- Suggest improvements and upgrades to hardware and software

- Modify commercial programs and customize them for internal needs
- Prepare computers for delivery to employees, loading them with the appropriate software and operating system

WEBMASTER

The responsibilities of the Webmaster are fragmenting. Once a jack-of-all-trades position responsible for the graphic design, content, hypertext markup language (HTML) programming, maintenance, and updates of a Web site, the Webmaster's job these days is much more specialized.

As e-commerce, Intranets, and Extranets have burst onto the scene, demanding more and more technical expertise on top of creative skills, a plethora of new Web-related job titles has emerged. Director of media integration, Internet sales engineer, and Extranet database specialist are just a few of the new positions. Director of electronic commerce has recently gone from rare to commonplace.

Webmaster Responsibilities

Although browsing the Net requires practically no training, constructing and maintaining enterprise-level Web sites requires enormous sophistication. The Webmaster serves as the central point of control for the design, administration, and maintenance of the Web site, sometimes including the Intranet and Extranet activities. The construction and maintenance of an enterprise's Web presence is overseen by a Webmaster, whose responsibilities include the following:

- **Outreach and Support.** Coordinate with publishers and content providers to encourage and assist the preparation of information resources, manage the first point of contact from the company regarding questions and user support, and coordinate training for publishers and server/browser administrators. The Webmaster is responsible for educating the users.

- **Navigation Management.** Design and deploy emerging strategies for promoting site navigation. Site navigation is quickly becoming the critical challenge for large Web sites that are composed of tens of thousands of individual pages.

- **HTTP Server Configuration.** Install and configure hypertext transfer protocol (HTTP) servers and set communications parameters that ensure delivery without delay. Establish served directory trees, segregating public files inside and private files outside. Convenient access by publishers should be provided to HTTP servers running under familiar operating systems so that publications are easily produced and visibility is controlled.

- **MIME Standardization.** Determine standard Multipurpose Internet Mail Extension (MIME) descriptors for all publications which are served, and see that servers and browsers are configured to produce and handle those MIME descriptors so that the site is visible in its various media to the largest possible audience.

- **WWW Browser Configuration.** Configure browsing parameters controlling file caching, font mapping, MIME awareness, and application launching so that users' browsing experiences are fluid, efficient, and productive.

- **Supporting Server Configuration.** Ensure that all supporting servers employed by WWW browsers (e.g., NNTP, SMTP, FTP, WAIS, X Windows, Gopher, Telnet) are properly installed and configured so that myriad Internet services are readily available to browsers.

- **Security Configuration.** Configure the network security layer to permit access to publications on a need-to-know basis so that publications are served to the intended audience with extremely high confidence of privacy and authenticity.

- **Primary HTML File Maintenance.** Maintain the home page, as well as a few layers of hypertext files directly surrounding it. Outer layers of hypertext and other types of published files should be maintained by the entire organization with the Webmaster as educator and consultant.

- **HTML Portability.** Promote proper use of Hypertext Markup Language (HTML), and stay abreast of developing HTML standards so that hypertext served from the Web site will look good through the eyes of all browsers and will employ the richest formatting techniques.

- **URL Portability.** Promote proper use of weakly qualified relative Uniform Resource Locators (URLs) so that published files can be ported to various platforms and directory trees with maximum ease.

- **Look-and-Feel Quality Management.** Present a consistent visual image on the Web site by promoting uniform fonts, formatting, icons, images, layout techniques, and modularization, including maintenance of HTML template and image archives. Determine appropriate compression techniques, resolutions, sizes, color maps, and depths to ensure that images—photographs and synthesized graphics—are delivered at sufficiently high speed and quality for intended output media.

- **Forms Interfacing.** Assist users who are creating HTML fill-out forms in processing responses into HTML output, and in managing the side effects of such processing. The Webmaster is not responsible for creating programs which process forms responses.

Webmaster Tasks

Much of the work of the Webmaster is repetitive and routine. After the exciting work of designing the Web site—including its goals, structure, pages and linkages, and incorporating new ideas and technologies into the site—comes the tedious task of maintaining it. The Webmaster needs to check for linkages, currency, updating databases, and correcting errors. At the same time, the Net is evolving rapidly. Webmasters already need to deal with the issue of databases and direct links to the Internet. More and more, they need to think about the implications of VRML (virtual reality markup language), Java (the client-side Net language), and server-side computing options. Adapting to the turbulent and changing Internet scene is not at all a routine task.

Routine Webmaster Roles

- Periodically check links to ensure they are current; change as needed.
- Update information in pages and databases.
- Check bugs and problems (e.g., nonworking pictures, maps, links, etc.); diagnose and fix them.
- Keep links to Internet up to date; search and find new links; add them.
- Structured Web development (e.g., adding staff links and linking the staff page).

Webmaster Competencies Required

- Ability to carry out basic Web browser functions, including Web search
- Ability to use a Web editor
- Ability to create and edit GIF and JPG pictures
- Ability to create transparent GIFs
- Ability to create clickable maps
- Basic fluency in HTML
- Ability to send edited work to Web server
- Ability to work with Web-connected database
- Understanding and ability to critique and develop Web's mission
- Understanding of Web as system
- Understanding of principles of good Web design
- Ability to assess new trends, formulate response strategies
- Ability to assess strengths and weaknesses of current Web implementation
- Willingness to subordinate own image of what Web should be to those of constituents

Nonroutine Webmaster Roles

- Work directly in creating and maintaining higher Web levels.
- Keep up with Internet literature and emerging trends and technologies.
- Conduct ongoing experimentation with emerging technologies.

A Sample Webmaster Job Description

There are as many job descriptions for Webmasters as there are Webmasters. This is not surprising for a role that is so aggressively evolving. Here is how one leading software company defines its Webmaster role.

Webmaster must be familiar with C, C++, Perl, Java, and VRML. Should be able to program forms and implement scripts. Ability to work with Mac, PC, and Unix environments, and to manage the Web site from a client as well as a server perspective. Oversee the technical management of the Web site, including integration of approved content onto the site, file management and site maintenance, database management and coordination of retrieval of pertinent information from the site to end-users, and archiving and record management.

Manage technical support for problems related to the Web site, program HTML and upload pages onto the site, and integrate multimedia assets and applications into the site. Total quality management of the site, including evaluation of links and usability. Help coordinate scripting and programming efforts with our Information Technology staff and other outside parties. Coordinate design implementation with creative staff and outside design teams, trying to match desired outcome with technological feasibility. Maintain the desired "look and feel" of the site. Generate weekly and monthly reports to executive staff using our Web Advantage technology.

Integrate new technologies (such as Acrobat Viewers) into the Web environment. Maintain cross-platform and cross-browser compatibility so that the Web site is accessible from a variety of different environments. Provide ongoing training and education. Prefer graduates in Computer Science or equivalent experience.

Advice to Budding Webmasters

- Be flexible and adaptable.
- Test new software on isolated systems.
- Be tidy and consistent to make troubleshooting easier.
- Security first.
- Work against viruses and hackers.
- Promote e-mail and its use.
- Stay on top of the business issues.

Webmaster Specialties

If you don't want to develop Internet applications but know how to create Web pages using HTML tools, there is a middle ground between hardcore C++ and Java programming and being a Web page master. Do you have enough technical skills to build and manage Web pages and work with the IT professionals who develop the Internet infrastructure? Examples:

Multimedia Design

The Web is a multimedia medium. It has created a host of new opportunities for graphic designers who want to move beyond traditional print media. What skills would you need to design the artwork for Web pages? How much of the technical HTML stuff do you need to know?

Web Page Designer

Web page designers are the persons who convert text documents to HTML format. These are usually not the only skills they have, and they sometimes refer to themselves as Webmasters. The latter should only be true if the person does the graphics design, text conversion, Web site setup, and maintenance. Otherwise, their only tasks involve designing the layout of the textual information and presenting it via HTML. However, they are required to work with the graphics designer and persons providing the content in order to provide quality Web pages. Web page designers also need to have knowledge of HTML, a browser, and good communication skills to accomplish their tasks.

Knowledge of HTML is the dominant educational requirement for Web page designers. HTML is a language that one can learn by reading a book. To be an efficient and productive Web page designer, one should also have skills in graphics design and some programming in Java and CGI.

Net Consultant

A Net consultant is a person who provides training and support to individuals, companies, and schools. They are considered experts in Internetworking, Web browsers, Web creations, installation, and maintenance. They have extensive knowledge of HTML, Java, CGI, VRML, and some scripting languages such as PERL. They must also be familiar with applications run on the Internet. In other words, they do it all! They are usually hired based on a reputation for getting the job done efficiently.

A degree in a technical field such as engineering or computer science is usually the education level for a consultant. However, since the Internet is such a new phenomenon, the majority of employees acquire their education from hands-on experience, either from working with companies that use the Internet or by self-taught methods. Since they are usually hired based on reputation, they would have to market themselves in order to establish a working relationship with a company.

Internet Specialist

This position requires skills in senior-level networking, LANs and WANs, the Internet, security, e-commerce, Unix, Windows NT, and Novell applications. You must be able to communicate effectively, possess an outgoing personality, and enjoy working with users. It's a high-level technical post; the next step up is team leader or manager.

Windows NT Systems Architect

Increasingly, IT shops are connecting via NT technology, making it imperative to have one person who can wrap his arms around the entire project and address topics like network design, network management, security, scalability and performance. You must have a background as a senior network engineer with solid NT troubleshooting skills, excellent detective abilities, and team-player attributes. The next stop on that very senior technical path is management.

Web Designer/Site Builder

To build the spiffiest site in the competitive marketplace, you'll need Web site development skills such as C++, Java, and HTML. You'll support the information, automation of customer service, help desk functions, ongoing development, and maintenance. You'll need a strong understanding of the business you'll be supporting and lots of intuition. People will constantly complain about the site, so strong prioritizing and customer service skills are also critical to your success in the position. But because of the high visibility of the job, your work won't go unnoticed. It usually involves project work, and consulting is common—it's a unique position. The next stop is the Web strategist's post.

Web Strategist

This position calls for a unique set of competencies—someone who has a strong understanding of the business, technical skills, and a marketing vision—to work with the Web site builder. You'll provide "sticky" Web content. You'll also keep an eye on the competition to maintain a leading edge. You'll work closely with the technical strategists and department heads to communicate the services effectively. It's the kind of high-visibility position that can open other technical leadership and strategy doors.

Web Site/Database Integrator

The Bureau of Labor Statistics expects 249,000 job openings in this area within the next ten years. Web site/database integrators will need to know standard Web site languages (HTML, PERL, C, Java, etc.), database languages (DB2, Oracle, SQL, etc.) and, in the case of legacy systems, some back-end knowledge of accounting packages, financial systems, and inventory systems. This job also requires the ability to hook the database(s) to an Internet site or an Intranet.

Web Developers

As the Internet continues to grow, so will the demand for Web developers. To land these jobs, you'll need to be well versed in a variety of programming languages including Java, Cold Fusion, C++ and PERL.

Internet Technologies Specialist: In Her Own Words

Beth Fleischer (*bfleischer@anhb.org*) is the Internet Technologies Specialist for the Alaska Federal Health Care Access Network, a federally funded telemedicine project. Fleischer has an undergraduate degree in architecture from Temple University. This is how she describes her job:

I am responsible for anything using Web-based technology that isn't the telecomm/network guy's stuff. I have designed and created a large, completely dynamic workplace called the Virtual Operating Environment which allows team members spread all over Alaska to communicate and work together. I am currently working on the Net site—since I am the only Web person on the team, I get to do it all, from site architecture and navigational design to coding. I designed the graphics for the site, and I have partial responsibility for content. I will also be involved in the selection and customization of software we choose for our store and forward system. I run my own Web servers and perform desktop/network support from the not-too-savvy office staff. I choose to work in smaller places—or places just establishing Intranet/Internet technologies—so I can do everything rather than being pigeon-holed into the programming aspect. Fun.

Best part of job? I love that the job has a tangible product that I produce and can show to people as My Work.

Worst part of job: Maintenance. In as many places as I can, I make the site self-maintaining—create interfaces for end users to change the news on the front page of the site, so I don't have to. Basically, I automate as much as I can, so I don't have to do boring maintenance.

Any surprises? The amount of schmoozing I have to do, and the number of meetings I have to attend, surprises me. I thought I might just get to sit at my desk and work, but not a chance.

What skills do you need more of? I want to learn XML, and I want to be a fabulous graphic artist. That being said, and the second being quite unlikely, I think I plan to move forward on learning XML. As far as non-technical skills, it's probably time to move into project management. I have the advantage of being able to understand each team member's job, because I was fortunate enough to do it all myself.

Technology Strategist

To perform this job, you'll need a breadth and depth of technical knowledge across all platforms. You'll need to focus on the future; be able to transition old technology to new systems; show expertise in networks, the Internet, operating systems, operations and applications; and demonstrate business savvy. Next stop is chief technology officer.

INTRANETMASTER

You've heard of a Webmaster? Intranets are the fastest-growing segment of the World Wide Web. So we think it won't be long before organizations will need people to handle the care and feeding of their increasingly mission-critical Intranets.

Just as corporate Web sites have become essential business tools, so have Intranets. There are dozens of definitions of Intranets being batted around. *Fortune Magazine* defined them as "private corporate networks that take advantage of the same basic properties as the Internet." Think of Intranets as tools employing Web technology that manage and distribute information to employees via their Web browsers. Ideally, they save time and improve efficiency, consistency, accountability, and communication.

The purpose of an Intranet is to track constantly changing information and make it available to users on a just-in-time (JIT) basis. Intranets are typically run from behind a company's firewall in a secure way so that it's only available to employees, partners, or other identified constituencies.

The Internet is identified with the World Wide Web, but just because it's the most conspicuous element of the Net, it is misleading to think that it is the only or even the biggest component of the Net. Like an iceberg whose mass is submerged beneath the surface, the Net has components that are deliberately hidden from public view but are the more powerful for it.

Most organizations committed to e-commerce have a three-tier Net strategy. The first tier is the Web, which operates outside the company's firewall and supports the company's Web site or e-business storefront. The second tier is the Intranet. Intranets are typically designed to create community for employees, providing services such as checking on retirement plans, submitting expenses, and scheduling vacations. The third tier is the Extranet. Extranets are places on the Net where a company's partners, distributors, and suppliers can price systems, configure systems, handle accounting, and otherwise conduct commerce.

For the most part, companies today rarely designate Webmasters for Intranets. But that will likely change as Intranets assume more significance and the Webmasters are stretched too thin by the responsibilities of managing three of the tiers. Companies are discovering that maintaining Intranets require time and bodies dedicated solely to that pursuit. So it's no wonder jobs are being redefined because of them.

Employee communication has ascended to top corporate priority, and the Intranet is the tool used to reach sprawling employee populations. Only a year ago, it was common to see nothing more than brochureware on a typical Intranet. Now there is real-time publishing, interactive business expense and retirement planning.

Pulling it off requires people who are not only competent about the technical details of the Intranet but handling the content or knowledge management. Knowledge experts are required to make sure information is not randomly put on the Intranet, but organized so that it's easily found and meaningful. Think of these critical Intranet players as information, technical, and content architects, all of whom are working together to make Intranets a delivery mechanism for the most critical and time-sensitive information employees generate and require. The goal is to make knowledge accessible and collaborative. This is no simple feat when you have hundreds—often thousands—of employees separated by walls and distance, yet they're all part of the same organization.

If you're interested in becoming an Intranet specialist, focus on understanding the capabilities of the Web and the tools needed to make it dynamic and elastic. Along with technical skills, polish your communication skills and especially learn about electronic publishing—quite different from the print variety.

APPLICATIONS

Interactivity/Usability Specialist

Building applications so that information flows seamlessly between systems requires analysts and programmers. Ensuring that information flows seamlessly between the systems and people is the work of interactivity/usability specialists. Interface work in the Net Economy usually concerns the browser, the most common Graphical User Interface (GUI). Interactivity/usability specialists deal with Web pages that have their own site-specific interfaces. The design goal is to make the interface as intuitive as possible. Interactivity design also applies to interactive multimedia educational products, virtual applications, and computer games.

Today, Net companies want to get away from the reputation of interaction design as "putting lipstick on a bulldog," or slapping an attractive interface on an ugly process. Trilogy Software puts it this way:

> Over the last three years, Trilogy's Human Computer Interface (HCI) group has become an essential part of creating and customizing Trilogy's products. We've changed our company's perception of interaction design from "prettying up interfaces" to "affecting the bottom line: revenue." Because of our position within the organization, each member of the HCI team receives unparalleled responsibility. As a result, each of us has been able to make a profound impact on our customers and products.

Interactivity/usability specialists at most Net companies should anticipate working with an integrated product development team to create interface solutions that empower users and tap the true potential of the company's technology. Typical activities include client interviews, prototyping sessions and presentations, and collaborative product development and specification. They often join multidisciplinary teams drawn from the fields of usability, psychology, interaction design, graphic design, information design, and computer science. Usability specialists' responsibilities include:

- Conducting fieldwork at customer sites to identify end-user goals and tasks
- Helping to create scenarios and storyboards, as well as paper and digital prototypes
- Applying appropriate usability techniques throughout the design/development process
- Running tests in the usability lab
- Reporting study results and making recommendations to interface designers and developers
- Gathering and analyzing feedback from end-users, customers, support and marketing
- Summarizing and analyzing research on relevant usability research

Typical skill-sets and requirements for interactivity/usability specialist include:

- Proven success in performing usability work
- Master's degree in psychology, human factors or a related field
- Command of a broad range of usability and design concepts (design experience a plus)
- Skill in interviewing and observation
- Expertise in a variety of techniques, such as formal usability testing, discount usability, heuristic evaluation, comparative testing, and surveys
- Training in data analysis
- Ability to communicate effectively verbally and in writing
- Experience with prototyping tools and Web-based applications

DEVELOPMENT (PROGRAMMING)

Developers

These days the term *programmer* is out of fashion. But let's face it—developers are just programmers with an attitude. In the old days, programmers were dissed because coding was considered grunt work; the real class was in analysis. Nowadays, the distinctions between coding and analysis are less discrete and relatively few developers do any real coding. They rely on code-generation tools, or they reuse existing code modules. Hence, the preferred descriptive title is *developer.*

Developers may be employed across business applications, systems, and network areas of information technology. Generically, a programmer's main responsibility is to translate a written specification of requirements prepared by an analyst or designer for a new or modified computer system, application, or network into a set of logical and exactly specified units or program specifications.

Typically, people working as developers would advance into designer and analyst roles after some years of experience. In some smaller organizations, all three roles may be vested in single individuals. Alternative titles have included Computer Systems Officer, Applications Programmer, and Systems Programmer, although several of these are shown in designations below.

Applications Developers typically write, test, and maintain computer programs to meet the application needs of end users in areas such as payroll or other accounting applications. This involves writing programs in fourth-generation languages (4GL), System Query Languages (SQL), and using other advanced software tools.

Network Developers work with vendor networking languages to support the implementation or modification of network configurations. Ongoing education in vendor products and knowledge in technical matters (such as ISDN, Broadband, modems, NT, LANs/WANs, Ethernet, bridges, and routers) is important.

Systems Software Developers work with the code used to define the particular operating system and sometimes also with low-level machine language. They write, maintain, and update programs that control the overall functioning of computers; assist in preparing specifications and user requirements; encode, test, debug, and document programs for relatively straightforward or small projects; and may assist programmer/analysts on more complex projects.

Database Developers are involved in the development of programs to suit access and maintenance of databases. It is often considered to be part of the database design role.

Communications Developers (systems) are involved in activities associated with programming telecommunications infrastructures, for example, stored program-controlled telephone exchanges. Communications programming (systems) has also been used to describe the work of network programmers.

Programmer/Analysts analyze user specifications and requirements; encode, test, debug, and document programs on large-scale, complex projects; and revise and update programs and documentation as required. Usually this requires four to six years relevant professional experience or an equivalent combination of education and experience.

By whatever name, computer developers generally undertake a number of tasks, the most common of which are:

- Assisting analysts and designers in researching and documenting computer users' requirements

- Analyzing objectives and problems specified by analysts and designers
- Using a particular programming language or machine code to convert design specifications into a set of step-by-step instructions (code) which can be directly interpreted by the computer and tested for correctness against desired results
- Preparing support documentation for other programmers, users of the system, and associated support services personnel
- Undertaking program design activities including data and module definition, specification of input/output between systems, and error message configurations
- Supervising, scheduling, and reporting on work of more junior programmers
- Modifying and documenting program code to correct errors or to enhance a program's capabilities
- Testing the validity and logic of programs and making amendments
- Preparing reports, manuals, and documentation on the status, operation and maintenance of system software for use by computer equipment suppliers, systems designers, other developers, and computer operators
- Undertaking analysis, review, and rewriting of programs and component modules of programs.

Requirements of Programmers

- High-level technical expertise in programming
- Logical approach to the solution of problems
- Self-reliant and capable of independent work
- Able to work well in a team
- Able to communicate with a variety of clients, peers, staff, and management
- Discipline in documentation of findings and work
- Willingness to continue to learn as technology changes

System Administrators—Unix

Organizations that rely on computing resources to carry out their mission have always depended on systems administration and systems administrators. The dramatic increase in the number and size of distributed networks of workstations in recent years has created a tremendous demand for more, and better trained, systems administrators. Understanding of the profession of systems administration on the part of employers, however, has not kept pace with the growth in the number of systems administrators or with the growth in complexity of system administration tasks. Both at sites with a long history of using computing resources and at sites into which computers have only recently been introduced, systems administrators face perception problems that present serious obstacles to their successfully carrying out their duties.

Systems administration is a widely varied task. The best systems administrators are generalists: they can wire and repair cables, install new software, repair bugs, train users, offer tips for increased productivity across areas from word processing to CAD tools, evaluate new hardware and software, automate a myriad of mundane tasks, and increase work flow at their site. In general, systems administrators enable people to exploit computers at a level that gains leverage for the entire organization.

Employers frequently fail to understand the background that systems administrators bring to their task. Because systems administration draws on knowledge from many fields, and because it has only recently begun to be taught at a few colleges, systems administrators may come from a wide range of academic backgrounds. Most get their skills through on-the-job training by apprenticing themselves to a more experienced mentor. Although the system of informal education by apprenticeship has been extremely effective in producing skilled systems administrators, it is poorly understood by employers and hiring managers, who tend to focus on credentials to the exclusion of other factors when making personnel decisions.

Junior Unix System Administrator

Besides high technical skills, the first order of business is strong interpersonal and communication skill. You must also be capable of explaining simple procedures in writing or orally and have good phone and e-mail manners. You should also be familiar with Unix and other operating systems and their commands/utilities. You should be able to edit files, use a shell, find users' home directories, navigate through the file system, and use I/O redirection. You must have a fundamental understanding of such functions as job control, soft and hard links, and the distinctions between the kernel and the shell. You will likely perform routine tasks under the direct supervision of a more experienced system administrator. You will also act as a front-line interface to users, accepting trouble reports and dispatching them to appropriate system administrators. Help desk experience is useful.

Desirable Background

- A degree or certificate in computer science or a related field
- Previous experience in customer support, computer operations, system administration, or another related area
- Motivated to advance in the profession

Senior Unix System Administrator

Employers look for strong interpersonal and communication skills: the ability to write proposals or papers, make presentations to customer or client audiences or professional peers, act as a vendor liaison, and work closely with upper management. You must have a solid understanding of a Unix-based operating system and an understanding of concepts such as paging and swapping, inter-process communication, devices and what device drivers do, and file system concepts (inode, superblock). You will likely use performance analysis to tune systems. You should also have a solid understanding of networking/distributed computing environment concepts, principles of routing, client/server programming, and the design of consistent network-wide file system layouts.

Appropriate responsibilities include:

- Designs/implements complex local and wide-area networks of machines
- Manages a large site or network
- Works under general direction from senior management
- Establishes/recommends policies on system use and services
- Provides technical lead or supervises system administrators, system programmers, or others of equivalent seniority
- Has purchasing authority and responsibility for purchase justification

Desirable Background

- A degree in computer science or a related field
- Extensive programming background in any applicable language
- Publications within the field of system administration
- Ability to solve problems quickly and completely
- Ability to identify tasks which require automation and automate them
- Ability to program in an administrative language (Tk, Perl, a shell), to port C programs from one platform to another, and to write small C programs

In addition to understanding the architecture of Unix, system administrators also need to work with Unix in the context of its place in the wider enterprise. To that end, if you have skills in the following disciplines, you will improve your negotiating position:

Local Environment Experience

- Specific operating systems, applications, or programming languages in use at the site
- SunOS
- AIX

- CAE/CAD software
- FrameMaker
- Mathematica
- Ada

Heterogeneity Experience

- Multiple Unix-based operating systems
- Running more than one Unix-based operating system
- Familiarity with both System V and BSD-based Unix operating systems
- Non-Unix operating systems (e.g., MS-DOS, Macintosh OS, or VMS)
- Internetworking Unix and other operating systems (MS-DOS, Macintosh OS, VMS)

Programming Skills

- Administrative language (Tk, Perl, a shell)
- Extensive programming experience in any applicable language

Networking Skills

- Configuring network file systems (for example, NFS, RFS, or AFS)
- Network file synchronization schemes (for example, rdist and track)
- Configuring automounters, license managers, NIS/NIS+
- TCP/IP networking protocols (ability to debug and program at the network level)
- Non-TCP/IP networking protocols (OSI, Chaosnet, DECnet, Appletalk, Novell Netware, Banyan Vines)
- High-speed networking (for example, FDDI, ATM, or SONET)
- Router-enabled TCP/IP networks
- Maintaining a site-wide modem pool/terminal servers
- X or X terminals
- Dial-up networking (SLIP, PPP, or UUCP)
- Configuring DNS/BIND
- Administering USENET news

Security

- Network security (building firewalls, deploying authentication systems, or applying cryptography to network applications)

- Multilevel classified environments
- Host security (passwords, uids/gids, file permissions, file system integrity)
- Third-party security packages

Site Specialties

- Sites with over 1,000 computers, over 1,000 users, or over a terabyte of disk space
- Sites with supercomputers
- Coordinating multiple independent computer facilities
- Sites with 100 percent uptime requirement
- Developing and implementing site disaster recovery plans
- Administering charge-back accounting

Databases

- Relational databases
- Database query language
- Object-oriented databases

Systems Analysis

Systems analysts are involved in the investigation, analysis, and specification of information systems. The analyst role is positioned in the systems development cycle between the initial business analyst stage and the detailed system design, build, and programming stage. Analyst staff are often drawn from designer and programmer personnel with some years of experience, although a qualification in some subject-matter area when supplemented by an appropriate IT diploma has also been a successful entry point for the role. In some organizations the distinction between analyst and designer is disappearing, although the designer/engineer must often be more conscious of technical matters than the analyst.

Modeling is one of the chief functions of analysts. They model processes. Systems analysts model information processes so that developers can render them into code. Business analysts model business processes to uncover opportunities for streamlining or reengineering. Market analysts model markets and the operations of buyers and sellers. Network analysts model the flow of packets among routers and hubs. Net analysts are responsible for modeling the various processes that support all the activities—e-mail, e-commerce, on-line auctions, comparison shopping, and so on—that constitute the Net initiatives of many companies. Many large enterprises classify systems analysts in the following designations:

Systems Analysts oversee the development process for new software and hardware. Projects could involve designing a new application program or other software. Systems analysts, on the other hand, may design either new hardware systems or software products. Systems analysts typically analyze, evaluate, and modify existing or proposed systems and related devices. They coordinate with users to ensure timely and efficient manufacturer's software release installation, and they design, encode, test, and debug programs or user-defined modifications.

Applications Systems Analysts generally focus on the building of a business application system once the business need has been defined and dimensioned by the business systems analyst. Alternative titles include Computer Systems Officer and Systems Officer. Typically, the applications systems analyst:

- uses data modeling to generate "IT solution scenarios" as a means of finding the optimum client solution.

- analyses system components, such as data flow, and defines the systems structures and inputs required to map out an IT technical solution.

- interfaces with the business systems analyst for clarification of client requirements.

- produces definitions, process flow documentation, output and processing rules and instructions as a basis for the work of designers and programmers.

- draws up a detailed design document for the system using suitable charts and diagrams, which indicates the various steps involved and describes the system in terms the client can understand.

- prepares other detailed documentation including hardware specifications and tender specifications.

- may be involved with client site installation activities.

Network Analysts are involved in the analysis of data movements, data flows, and technical requirements to define a network strategy and the equipment required to meet projected data traffic. Network analysis includes the following tasks:

- Investigating the physical space requirements for network equipment
- Dimensioning and planning the network size, capacity, and configuration
- Interfacing with network system management to ensure client needs are met
- Working with network designers and developers to build and implement network solutions

Operations Systems Analysts typically analyze the components of operational systems to optimize system performance against operational standards in areas such as response time and down time. The focus is on operational systems such as mainframes (MVS, VSE), midrange (Unix, Windows NT, AIX, AS/400), and desktop solutions (Windows 98).

Information Architect. In the brick-and-mortar world an architect designs structures. In the virtual world, information architects are responsible for defining the rules and operating principles that organize a company's information technology. In many ways, the architectures they create are the crown jewels of a company's value. The Net itself is an architecture. Every company has someone who serves as the chief architect, although they may be named something else. For example, Sun Microsystems calls some of the people who function as architects "principal investigators." By whatever name, architects typically research and prototype systems in an effort to generate a long-term technical infrastructure or strategy. An information architect is part builder, part librarian. Information architects clarify the mission and vision of a document, balancing the needs of an organization and the needs of its audiences. They are responsible for learning how users find information in a site by defining the site's organization, navigation, and labeling systems.

Requirements of Analysts

- Able to think logically and analytically in a problem-solving environment
- Capable of imaginative abstract reasoning
- Able to work well in a team environment
- Self-reliant and capable of independent work
- Clarity in written and verbal communications
- Able to accept responsibility
- Thorough knowledge of the relevant specialty area
- Willingness to continuously update personal IT skill and knowledge

OPERATIONS

Computer Operations Manager

- Manages all activities related to the operations and maintenance of mainframe computer and peripheral equipment
- Analyzes usage patterns and establishes schedules and procedures for maximum utilization of the system
- Coordinates activities with other IT areas and other departments
- Normally reports to the information technology manager

Computer Operations Supervisor

- Supervises computer operation, scheduling, and distribution of mainframe data processing operations
- Analyzes operating instructions and user needs to establish operating procedures and production schedules
- Typically reports to data processing operations manager

Computer Operator

- Operates, monitors, and controls a mainframe computer and related peripheral equipment using established procedures
- Monitors console or terminal, storage devices and printers, and reports problems or variances
- May assist in reconfiguring system components when individual units fail
- Typically reports to data processing operations supervisor

Computer Operator—Senior

- Operates, monitors, and controls a mainframe computer and related peripheral equipment
- Monitors console or terminal, storage devices, and printers and reports problems or variances
- Analyzes operating instructions to determine equipment settings and operating procedures
- Reconfigures systems components when individual units fail. Maintains machine performance and production records
- Typically reports to data processing operations supervisor

Data Entry

- Enters and verifies a variety of data in appropriate formats
- Tracks and verifies quality of data entry from all sources
- Resolves problems regarding the data
- Typically reports to the data entry supervisor

Data Entry Supervisor

- Supervise and monitors the quality of the data entry process
- Resolves data integrity issues and coordinates with other areas of IT

Help Desk Specialist

- Responds to inquiries and request for assistance with the organization's computer systems or PCs

- Identifies problem, troubleshoots, and provides advice to assist users

- Coordinates with other IT areas to resolve problems if necessary

- May operate in a mainframe or microcomputer environment

NETWORKING

Networking may be the most in-demand IT specialty. A majority of the HR professionals interviewed for this book cited networking as the highest growth area within their IT departments. Candidates aspiring to these positions need to comprehend communication and information at a much higher and more complex level. They will need to be knowledgeable in Internet, voice, data, and cable capabilities as they come together in the next few years.

Network Support

Networking is the hottest area of *Internet* jobs and we can easily spend the rest of the book looking at the ins and outs of this space. Network support jobs can be categorized as network infrastructure support, network operating system support, and Web support.

Network Infrastructure support has to do with the physical structure of the Net. Someone has to make and connect cables to the routers, hubs, and switches that make up the Net. Someone has to do the troubleshooting and testing, but this area of the job market is increasingly perceived as having less value than the skills required to extend the Net through software. Network devices with which you should be familiar include:

- Bridges
- Gateways
- Hubs
- Modems
- Repeaters
- Routers
- Switches

Hardware disciplines in this area include:

- Authentication
- Capacity planning

- Directory services
- File and table management
- Firewalls install and terminate cable
- Network resource optimization
- Network security
- Resource sharing
- Testing

Standards and protocols in this area include:

- Asynchronous Transfer Mode
- Domain Name Service (DNS)
- Ethernet
- Frame Relay
- ISDN
- Lightweight Directory Access Protocol (LDAP)
- Network Information Services (NIS)
- PPP
- Simple Network Management Protocol (SNMP)
- Telecommunications (T1, T2, T3, etc.)

Cisco Systems is the 800–pound gorilla in this aspect of networking. Obtaining the Cisco Certified Internetwork Expert (CCIE) certification is a highly desirable credential if you aspire to a career in any area of Net networking. Consult the *Internet Jobs!* Web site for links to Cisco certification providers.

Network Infrastructure Competencies Required

- Install and terminate cable
- Test cables
- Monitor network for performance
- Install communications hardware
- Configure communications hardware (modems, routers, gateways, repeaters, and bridges)
- Configure and analyze network analysis
- Monitor security reports and alerts
- Demonstrate knowledge of protocol architecture
- Test configurations and troubleshoot problems

- Develop contingency plans
- Design network topology

Network Operating System support has to do with managing a network operating system (NOS), an operating system that controls hardware and schedules software on a network so it can be available to many people. Having a critical mass of competencies in these skill sets is essential to any company hoping to compete in the Net Economy.

Network Operating System Support Competencies Required

- Install and terminate cable
- Test cables
- Monitor network for performance
- Install communications hardware
- Configure communications hardware (modems, routers, gateways, repeaters, and bridges)
- Configure and analyze network analysis
- Monitor security reports and alerts
- Demonstrate knowledge of protocol architecture
- Test configurations and troubleshoot problems
- Develop contingency plans
- Design network topology

Web support is perhaps the hottest classification for network jobs. The World Wide Web is the fastest growing segment of the Internet. Worldwide Internet commerce will top $1 trillion by 2003, according to a report by International Data Corp. The Framingham, Massachusetts-based research firm estimates that more consumers buying online, larger dollar amounts per transaction, and increased business-to-business purchases on the Web account for most of that growth. Almost all of this growth will take place over the Web. The most critical standards and protocols in this area include:

- Apple Appletalk
- Banyan Vines
- Domain Name Service
- Lightweight Directory Access Protocol (LDAP)
- Microsoft Network
- Network Information Services (NIS)

- Novell NetWare
- Simple Network Management Protocol (SNMP)
- TCP/IP

Certification is available for Banyan (Certified Banyan Specialist and Certified Banyan Engineer, Novell (Certified Novell Administrator), and Microsoft (Microsoft Certified Systems Engineer). In addition Learning Tree International offers certification programs in Local Area Networks, Wide Area Networks, NetWare, TCP/IP, and Windows NT.

Web Support Competencies Required

- Install and terminate cable
- Test cables
- Monitor network for performance
- Install communications hardware
- Configure communications hardware (modems, routers, gateways, repeaters, and bridges)
- Configure and analyze network analysis
- Monitor security reports and alerts
- Demonstrate knowledge of protocol architecture
- Test configurations and troubleshoot problems
- Develop contingency plans
- Design network topology

Networking Specialties

LAN Administrator. Installs, configures, and maintains the organization's LAN server and workstations. Manages performance and maintains security of LANS. Works with multiple hardware and software platforms at an intermediate level. Acts as primary organizational interface with vendor and provides internal analysis and support. Manages performance of a multiple hardware and software platform interface at the most complex level. Reports to an IT operations manager.

LAN/WAN Manager. Manages the acquisition, installation, and maintenance of the organization's local area networks and wide area networks. Analyzes products and recommends use of new products and services to senior management. Manages LAN/WAN performance and security. Establishes and implements policies and procedures for LAN/WAN usage throughout the organization. May manage only LAN or WAN area. Typically reports to an IT executive.

Voice Communications. Designs, programs, installs, and maintains voice technology systems, including switching systems, voice mail, cellular, and paging equipment. Analyzes business needs, researches, and recommends solutions.

Network Specialist. Keeps everyone connected. Makes sure people in the company get the information they need when they need it, and keeps unwanted users out of the system. Using cable, fiber optics, or even wireless communications, connects users to the company's computer system. Has a thorough understanding of current networking technology for local area networks (LANs), metropolitan area networks (MANs), wide area networks (WANs), and the Internet. Identifies and documents problems, causes, and ramifications.

The network specialist continually assesses the current system to make sure it meets the needs of the company, and charts network traffic and downtime to help plan for the future. He or she documents the network configuration, prepares backup plans and procedures, and installs upgrades with a minimum of disruption to the network.

Network specialists are responsible for the security and administration of the networks that are now prevalent in many companies. They also design and implement systems that keep networks functioning in the event of a power failure or other emergency. Larger companies often employ several network specialists, each of whom performs a different function. In smaller companies one or two people do everything relating to network administration and maintenance. Other duties include:

- planning for and then installing the hardware and software that comprise the network.
- adding and deleting files to the network server.
- maintaining the printers and other peripherals connected to the network.
- setting up user accounts and access.
- training staff to use the hardware and software that make up the network.
- troubleshooting problems and questions encountered by staff members.

Technology is changing rapidly, and you need to stay informed of recent developments, new products, and emerging communication strategies and methods. As the world gets wired, you're sure to be in hot demand. The Bureau of Labor Statistics' *1998–99 Occupational Outlook Handbook* reported 65,000 current openings and projected hires over the next twelve months for network specialists.

Network Security Specialist duties include:

- regulating access to various computer files.
- monitoring file use to make sure that only authorized users can access particular files.

- changing passwords.

- maintaining and changing employee information and ensuring its confidentiality.

- backing up files to guarantee their safety in the event of problems to the network.

Network Systems Technician monitors reliability of network infrastructure and operating systems on multiple platforms; diagnoses and repairs problems.

Data Communications Analyst designs, installs, and maintains data communication between mainframe, terminals, printers, LANS, and remote site hardware.

Internetwork Engineer

Network Installers perform LAN installation, router/firewall installation, and setup FTP sites. They have skills in a wide assortment of router products, know how to set and recover passwords, have experience with downloading Operating Systems images and configuration files via FTP servers, and have knowledge of file architecture of routers. These persons also provide troubleshooting capabilities for companies. In other words, they provide the installation and customer support for a company.

Basic knowledge of networking and protocols is necessary. Therefore, having courses that cover this would be a plus. Many persons have a degree in Computer Science, Electrical Engineering, or a combination of the two. At least a background in computer hardware and software would be sufficient. There are some companies that offer certification for Internetworking.

Protocol Designer

The persons who define the Internet services are called the Protocol Designers. They write protocols for e-mail, File Transfer Protocol (FTP), Telnet, USENET News, Gopher, and Hypertext Transfer Protocol (HTTP). These persons should have knowledge of existing protocol, the creativity to design or modify protocols, the ability to test the protocols, and experience with networking. Many of them have performed or do perform Internetwork Engineering tasks as well. Most Protocol Designers have an educational background in Electrical Engineering and/or Computer Science. A number of technical schools offer one- or two-year programs of courses to be certified in writing protocols.

Networking Competencies Required

- Networking Skills

- Internet Basics

- PC Hardware Fundamentals

- PC Operating Systems

- Information System Concepts
- Information Technology or Computer Science
- Programming
- Systems Analysis
- Systems Design
- Database Design
- Networking Essentials
- Network Fundamentals
- Internetworking and LAN Management
- Wide Area Networking
- TCP/IP Fundamentals

Chief Network Administrator: In Her Own Words

Kristina M. is the chief network administrator for a large insurance company just taking its first baby steps on the Web. Kristina has a graduate degree in Linguistics and a B.S. in Applied Science and Technology. Before taking this job, she spent two years as a senior network administrator for an ISP and three years as computer lab network manager for a university.

Responsibilities? I oversee the security, operation, and integrity of Web, mail, DNS, FTP, and other servers and routers. Configure, maintain, and troubleshoot Web and database servers. Serve as general last-resort troubleshooting help. Research new technologies, write code for Web-based applications.

Required skillset? Perl/Unix shell/some C programming, Web server configuration and maintenance (NT and Unix). Knowledge of TCP/IP routing, OSPF, Rip, BGP. Configuration and administration of Cisco, Ascend, and Livingston routers and dialup access servers, CSU/DSU's, Frame Relay, PRI/BRI, system security, database design and administration. Operating systems and networking such as Unix (BSDI, FreeBSD, IRIX, AIX, Solaris, Linux), Windows NT, Windows 95, network troubleshooting, firewalls, packet filters.

Best part of the job? Learning something new every day and having a chance to play with new technologies or even just a new coding problem.

Worst part of the job? Dealing with people who refuse to learn and don't want to learn anything. There is often difficulty explaining to some end users that something isn't possible or feasible given the time allotted to a project.

DATABASE JOBS

Database Administrator

The database administrator (DBA) is responsible for the care and feeding of the enterprise's data. It is your job to determine the best way to organize, manage, store, and dispose of data. You will design reports and forms to present the information your customers need, make changes, and test everything before it's put on the shelf. To keep your data secure and protected from catastrophic events, you create and perform backup and recovery processes. With your creativity and skills in organization, communication, and attention to detail, your customers always find what they need. The Microsoft Skills 2000 July 1998 Skills Gap Survey reported 51,000 current openings and projected hires over the next twelve months in the area of database administrations. DBAs typically:

- oversee the technical design, development, and maintenance of databases and master files on large complex projects.
- design, implement, and maintain moderately complex databases.
- maintain database dictionaries and ensure system integration.
- maintain database dictionaries, ensure database performance, and resolve problems.
- coordinate with IT departments to ensure implementation and monitoring of databases.
- analyze and project long-range space requirements.
- work with Database Analysts and others on complex projects.

Database Specialists design, install, update, modify, maintain, and repair computer databases. There are a variety of database specialists. Unless they work for a very small company, they are usually part of a project group or team. Members of the project team may specialize in different aspects of working with data. Database administrators code, test, and install new databases. They also modify existing databases by developing new programming code. Database design analysts design new databases and coordinate their development. Frequently they work with clients on custom projects. Duties usually include:

- providing technical support for existing databases.
- modifying existing databases as circumstances change.
- customizing commercial databases for specific needs.
- planning and designing databases for new clients.
- solving problems to meet the needs of clients.

- programming databases for a wide variety of applications.
- overseeing the installation of new databases.
- training staff in client companies about the use of new or existing databases.

IT ADMINISTRATION

Information Technology Administration is an upcoming field in the Net Economy, according to an *InformationWeek* survey of more than 3,400 of these professionals. Salaries are up and bonuses are generous because of technology-hungry companies looking to beef up IT administration as they move more and more initiatives to the Net. The survey found:

- Salaries rose 14.5 percent or $7,000 between 1997 and 1998, a trend that continues today. The average salary for IT administrators is $55,000, up from $48,000.
- Database administrators command the highest average salaries at over $63,000, followed by systems administrators ($55,400), and network administrators ($51,460). Pay is typically higher at larger companies than at small and midsized ones.
- Most administrators feel secure in their current positions, given the abundance of job prospects as evidenced by the persistent calls they get from recruiters. Two-thirds describe their job security as above average.

The biggest challenge for IT administrators is to make the decision to stay technical or to move into management. Staying current in technology is a full-time job, and deepening one's technical expertise is rewarded at most Net companies, but the market is also biased toward a management track, and many IT administrators feel pressure to pursue a project management track in order to advance financially. Progressive companies recognize that it is in their interests to ensure that their star technical performers are not left behind financially. Otherwise they will bolt to new opportunities or, worse, accept management positions for which they are neither qualified nor enthusiastic.

Information Technology Director

Directs IT operations, including computer operations, technical support, systems analysis, and programming. May also direct database management, telecommunications, IT training, and microcomputer technology. Establishes technical priorities, standards, and procedures. Ensures sufficient systems capacity for organizational needs. Typically reports to the Chief Operating Officer in large companies and the Chief Executive Officer in medium-sized companies. This is typically a position at companies with more than 1,000 employees and more than $200 million in revenues.

Information Technology Manager

Oversees IT operations, including computer operations, technical support, systems analysis, and programming; may also direct other IT areas. Establishes technical priorities, standards, and procedures. Ensures sufficient systems capacity for organizational needs. This is the top-level IT job in small organizations (less than 1,000 employees and $200 million in revenues) and the second- or third-level job within large organizations.

PC Support Specialist

Analyzes, plans, designs, and installs new personal computer systems and reviews, monitors, and upgrades existing personal computer systems. Determines user specifications for hardware and software. Oversees the planning, installation, control, and maintenance of personal computers within the organization. Analyzes business needs and new technology and makes recommendations. Develops organizational policies and procedures for hardware and software acquisition and use. Purchases or builds software to meet user needs. Installs new and maintains existing hardware and software. Typically reports to LAN/WAN manager or PC support manager.

Systems Project Manager

Plans, organizes, and controls analysis of computer system requirements and development of procedures for implementation, programming and maintenance of major computer systems. Coordinates efforts with other IT departments and users. Ensures that project timelines and budgets are met.

Internet CEO

This individual will be invaluable to the company that is beyond early-stage start-up. This person will need fifteen to twenty years of industry experience and three to five years of experience as a general manager or CEO running a significant business. The most likely talent pool will come from technology and new media.

E-Commerce Manager

Electronic commerce continues to be the hottest new trend in IT services, and the manager of e-commerce serves a crucial role. This individual will be responsible for creating linked networks, databases, and business solutions. Because Web technology is changing constantly, and electronic commerce is relatively new, those candidates who are able to identify emerging trends will continue to have enormous potential.

Online Community Manager

You will be responsible for building, growing, and maintaining a thriving on-line community. You'll need to implement and manage e-mail, instant messaging, chat, message boards, and other community-building initiatives that help draw visitors to the site.

Computer Security

There's plenty of job security in IT security jobs. Unfortunately for most of us, computer security is a growth industry because of the ever-increasing threat from hackers, computer viruses, and other attacks. The goal of computer security is to protect the confidentiality, integrity, and availability of information systems, including the applications and data on the Web. Not long ago only large corporations needed to concern themselves with IT security issues. Their effort to keep information proprietary was the main focus of the field. This is no longer the case. Technology has become so prevalent that it affects almost every aspect of daily life. Computers are at the core of most businesses, ranging from trading systems used on the stock exchanges to the financial Web page that delivers yesterday's closing prices. Web security concerns the same three issues:

Confidentiality is the concept that information is unavailable to those who are unauthorized to access it. Strict controls must be implemented to ensure that only those persons who need access to certain information have that access. In some situations, such as those with confidential and secret information, people should only have access to that data which is necessary to perform their job function. Many computer crimes involve compromising confidentiality and stealing information. The concept of allowing access to information or resources only to those who need it is called "access control."

Integrity ensures that information cannot be modified in unexpected ways. Loss of integrity could result from human error, intentional tampering, or even catastrophic events. The consequences of using inaccurate information can be disastrous. If improperly modified, data can become useless, or worse, dangerous. Efforts must be made to ensure the accuracy and soundness of data at all times.

Availability prevents resources from being deleted or becoming inaccessible. This applies not only to information, but also to networked machines and other aspects of the technology infrastructure. The inability to access those required resources is called a "denial of service." Intentional attacks against computer systems often aim to disable access to data, and occasionally the aim appears to be the theft of data. These attacks are launched for a variety of reasons, including both political and economic motivations. In some cases, electronic mail accounts are flooded with unsolicited messages, known as "spam" mail, to protest or further a cause. Additionally, these attacks could be an integral part of a coordinated effort, such as bringing down a home banking system.

In general, the responsibilities of computer security are to:

- develop information security strategy and plans.
- perform risk assessments.
- develop the security architectures.
- create and install security tools.
- manage partnerships.

Therefore the roles that are required include:

- strategy and planning specialists.
- risk assessment specialist.
- security architecture specialist.
- security designers (system and programming skills).
- security administrators.

Security at most modern Web-based companies is a very big deal. The brand a company like eBay or E*Trade has spent millions of dollars developing can be destroyed instantly by a hacker who succeeds in penetrating the system's defenses. For that reason, companies have evolved elaborate security structures. Here is the computer security hierarchy at a Fortune 500 company with substantial legacy investments at a Web component:

- Chief information security officer
- Policy administration, awareness
- MVS security (technical, networks, administrative)
- Unix security (technical, networks, administration)
- Microcomputer security (technical, administration)
- Internet/Intranet security
- Security help desk
- Business recovery (data center DR)
- Physical security (all platforms)
- Security quality assurance
- Security research (architecture)

Data Security Specialists

Data security specialists are concerned with the protection of a company's computer-based information banks. Security problems have intensified with the proliferation of networks, since skilled hackers from outside an organization have increasingly been able to gain access to internal networks. Data security specialists need to keep information safe from many perils, including floods, fire, power outages, fraud, theft, invasion of privacy, and viruses.

To perform their jobs effectively, data security specialists need experience in technical areas such as programming, systems analysis, and telecommunications. They must also understand the company's business in order to know what computerized functions the company cannot afford to lose. Working alone or in teams, data security specialists set up security procedures to protect vulnerable information. Sometimes they, or outside consultants, conduct "raids" on the system during which they try to expose security loopholes. This kind of testing is designed to expose weaknesses in the security system.

Data Security Auditors

Like data security specialists, auditors in the computer industry are also concerned with security issues, but their main job is to ensure that all aspects of a company's information systems function as designed. Auditors inspect programs, systems, operational procedures, documentation, control techniques, disaster plans, insurance protection, and fire protection.

Auditors sometimes audit "through the computer." This action involves verifying the accuracy of a computer program by using sample data to test processing accuracy and control procedures that are built into the program. They may also audit "around the computer" by examining computer input and output to make sure these are accurate. Frequently auditors use a test program or audit software package to make their tests. They can then compare the results of the audit program with the output of the company's programs. In making such comparisons, they may uncover unauthorized changes in company's programs that could be evidence of fraud. If they uncover discrepancies, auditors report these to upper management. They may also make recommendations for changes to ensure system integrity and accuracy. These recommendations are frequently carried out by data security specialists.

Information Security Technical Specialist

These technical specialists assist with the design, implementation, and administration of security solutions in a distributed systems environment. Other requirements include:

- familiarity with mainframe and open systems architectures.
- maintaining and coordinating security software systems.
- providing maintenance, problem resolution, and analysis of security exposures and opportunities on multiple platforms, such as Unix, Intranet/ Internet, MVS, Tandem, Unisys, or network firewalls and security servers.
- ability to identify and prioritize issues and provide customer service.

Security Architect

This specialist provides architectural oversight and direction for enterprise-wide security technology. Other requirements include:

- ability to ensure high-level integration of IT systems development with security policies and information protection strategies.
- knowledge of industry direction and emerging security standards, especially those concerning public key infrastructure, data warehousing, object-oriented technology, and global networking.

Information Security Analyst

Information security analysts assist in developing and maintaining an integrated program to protect the integrity, confidentiality, and availability of the company's information resources on a worldwide basis. Primary responsibilities of this position include support of the virus containment center, assisting in the development of assigned security initiatives, and developing knowledge of security technologies, issues, and direction. Essential job functions include:

- Maintaining the virus containment center to provide adequate protection from viruses.
- Developing information protection procedures and guidelines to support various aspects of the company's worldwide information protection program.
- Identifying security risks and exposures by participating in security reviews, evaluations, and risk assessments.
- Designing and developing security and control measures to address identified risks.
- Providing ongoing consulting assistance domestically and internationally in addressing security issues and implementing security policies, procedures, and measures.
- Strengthening overall knowledge of security issues, technologies, and direction.

Cross-Platform Security Specialist

A cross-platform security specialist adds value to heterogeneous organizations by minimizing the security seams between applications. Typically, different systems and applications require different passwords and log-on processes, making navigation between these systems difficult for users from a security perspective. The primary responsibility is to administer security between and among platforms to minimize opportunities for compromises in security while keeping the usability experience high. For shops that favor single sign-on, a process that gives authorized users the ability to sign on only once and then have access to all authorized resources, you will need to be familiar with security packages such as IBM's RACF or such enterprise management tools as CA's Unicenter TNG.

You will need to function as the resident end-to-end network and data security specialist. The job requires a strong networking background, firewall expertise, and the ability to make the applications safe but not too cumbersome. If you have a strong background in applications programming, network technology, the Internet, and security, this is the job for you. Depending on your ability to sell your concepts, the next stop may be technology strategist.

Information Security Principal

An information security principal assists in developing and maintaining an integrated information protection program to protect the integrity, confidentiality, and availability of the company's information resources on a worldwide basis. General responsibilities of this position include developing and supporting assigned security initiatives, assisting in the identification of security issues and requirements for the company, and maintaining current knowledge of security technologies issues and directions. Essential job functions include:

- Developing information protection policies, procedures, strategies, and architectures to define and support the company's worldwide information protection program, including direction, activities, and responsibilities.

- Conducting security reviews, evaluations, risk assessments, and develops recommendations for improvements as appropriate.

- Developing and presenting ongoing security awareness and training information to employees, management, and information custodians to ensure that security responsibilities are understood.

- Evaluating security and control aspects of new technologies and defining security requirements.

- Designing security and controls for new technologies to address such areas as infrastructure, security administration, user identification and authentication, access to data, monitoring, and reporting.

- Developing and implementing business continuity planning policies and procedures, and providing direction and assistance in the development of business continuity plans.

- Assisting in maintaining the virus containment center to ensure that adequate protection and response to viruses is provided.

SAP Security Subject Matter Expert (SME)

SAP is a popular enterprise resource planning application with a security component. This position administers SAP R/3 security for selected Infinity environments. You participate in evaluation and refinement of global SAP security procedures and standards for Infinity pilot sites and provide knowledge transfer of those procedures to on-site security staff at pilot locations. You also provide security administration as required for pilot bites during the development phase of the project. Essential job functions include:

- Responding to client requests to create user IDs, modify or create user and group profiles, define authorizations, change passwords, and modify security elements within the SAP systems.

- Evaluating SAP global security procedures and standards from the administrative perspective and assisting in refining them to improve the overall global security environment.

- Providing SAP security administration when a site begins the pilot development phase of SAP R/3.

- Training on-site operations staff in the security procedures required to support the production environment. Providing training materials, documentation, and assistance to accomplish this end.

- Providing assistance to each Infinity pilot site as necessary until transfer of administration occurs successfully.

- Working within a team environment continually to enhance and improve security implementation at international pilot sites.

Security specialists with skill sets in the following areas are especially desirable:

- Intranet/Extranet Security
- Penetration Testing
- Public Key Infrastructure
- Private Key Encryption
- Virtual Private Networks
- Intrusion Detection Systems

TESTING AND MAINTENANCE

Quality Assurance

Quality assurance specialists evaluate and test new software programs to make sure they work as designed. Programs are evaluated against designer specifications and user requirements. Such evaluation of new programs usually uncovers bugs and leads to further revisions and modifications. Quality assurance specialists serve under a variety of titles, such as "software quality" and "software quality assurance."

Quality assurance jobs are process-oriented, focusing on preventing defects. Quality assurance professionals develop the procedures a company follows to develop and maintain software, predict the number of bugs and predict the effects of development methods on quality. They also explain quality's bottom-line impact to managers.

Quality Assurance Competencies

Depending on the level, requirements may include knowledge of:

- Software processes
- Measurement
- Inspections
- Standards

  SPICE (an international collaborative effort to develop a standard in the area of software process assessment)

  European Strategic Programme of Research into Information Technology (ESPRIT),

  ISO9000-3 (the ISO-9000 standard for software)

  Capability Maturity Module; software process standards established by companies such as Motorola, AT&T, and Bell Laboratories; and military standards.

To test new programs, quality assurance specialists spend time using the programs in a way that simulates how the average user would use them. For example, if they are testing a new game, they will play it over and over for hours, trying to make it crash or stop working. They also keep track of what they do, so if the program does crash, they can reconstruct the sequence of moves or commands that led to the crash. Some QA specialists also work closely with programmers. After evaluating the product, they meet with programmers to describe the problems they encountered and suggest ways for solving glitches. They might also offer ideas to make a program more fun, lively, user-friendly, or entertaining.

Some quality assurance specialists work directly with customers who are experiencing problems with software they have purchased. In these cases, they listen to customers' complaints and try to understand what sequence of commands led to the problem that is being reported. They then try to duplicate the problem in the lab in order to conduct more in-depth tests and diagnose the bug.

Some companies are trying to automate the QA process. But even when they do, they still need a human technician to administer and monitor the automated tests as well as to interpret the results of the tests and write up conclusions and recommendations. More experienced QA specialists work as quality assurance analysts. In this position, they write and revise the QA standards or specifications for new programs. They also create the quality assurance tests that technicians use to evaluate programs. Creating such tests generally involves computer programming. Some analysts also evaluate proposals for new software products in order to decide whether the proposed product is capable of doing what it is supposed to do.

Software Testing

Software testers are product-oriented; they are concerned with eliminating defects. They focus on business requirements and the ability to understand those requirements, and they develop test scenarios that ensure that those requirements are met. In some companies, testers are responsible for defining a process to manage defects. Their tasks include test-plan generation, doing inspections and walk-throughs, picking tools, designing processes, collecting metrics, and doing benchmark calibration. They operate under such job titles as Testing Specialist, Director of Software Testing, Test Manager, occasionally Quality Assurance Specialist, and more recently, Year 2000 Specialist and International Standards Organization (ISO) Inspector.

Software Testing Competencies

- Defect estimation
- Measurement
- Inspections and testing methods

6
Business Jobs

Leadership is a potent combination of strategy and character. But if you must be without one, be without the strategy.

—*General H. Norman Schwartzkopf*

BUSINESS FIRST

The central point of this book is to remember that Net jobs are created and sustained by businesses. E-business, after all is said and done, is simply business by another name. The result is an insatiable demand for business-savvy people with different skill sets. As enterprise dependence on information technology in general and the Net in particular grows, even heavy-duty IT types will find themselves increasingly drawn into business decisions. The more comfortable you are with the business side of your job, the more successful you will be. It's as simple as that.

To educate yourself on all aspects of e-business, you can get an MBA, read a stack of books, conduct some focus groups, get an internship in a marketing group, and take courses and seminars. All of these are good ideas, but it's probably overkill for a Webmaster to take a few years off to get an MBA. It's unnecessary because everything you need to learn is probably within a few hundred yards from where you will work. It's a matter of attitude. Are you willing to do what it takes to get your mind around the fundamental principles driving e-business? The emphasis, don't forget, is on how to move your career into an e-business focused world. As more and more companies develop e-business strategies, the need for competent, knowledgeable employees will also grow.

Let's take a good look at the business jobs that support every Net enterprise. If you can understand the business skills driving these jobs, you can make a real difference. Few technically oriented people come by these skills naturally, but they can all be learned, and learning them will make all the difference in your e-business career.

Account Development

Account development bridges marketing and sales, offering candidates the large responsibility of owning a customer account through the sales cycle. Account developers research industry trends, develop the business case, and provide value by fitting company products to clients' business problems. Other responsibilities include presenting company technology to senior executives, converting leads into active sales cycles by creating client urgency, and prepping the account for an easy contract closing.

Attributes Required of Account Development Managers

- Creativity and ability to think out of the box
- Entrepreneurial spirit: aggressiveness and tenacity
- Good problem-solving skills
- Strong analytical abilities

Advertising and Public Relations

Advertising and public relations, like most other marketing careers, require people skills and a growing savvy on the use of Net resources. Advertising and PR jobs require the individual to work closely with a client base who can be difficult and demanding. Advertising and PR are not for the faint of heart. Continual deadlines can cause high levels of stress and pressure. The advertiser may have to work all night or weekends to ensure that a presentation is properly prepared to meet a pressing deadline.

Probably no other marketing career requires greater communication skills than does a career in advertising. Excellent copywriting skills are a must for the entry-level advertising or PR job. The advertising and PR person must also be able to make a very professional presentation that is persuasive yet flexible.

Creativity? You better believe it. A successful advertiser will be the individual who can create a commercial message that the consumer will remember. Do you remember the Energizer Bunny who keeps going and going and going? Somebody's career was made with that commercial series.

Competition for beginning advertising and PR jobs is intense. There are many more candidates than most advertising positions. You must be willing to start at the bottom and work your way up. An internship in the advertising field is a must. Many of these internships will not pay, so be prepared to struggle financially. However, the experience should greatly improve your chances in entering the advertising field.

Bad news: starting pay is probably going to be low. Remember the inexorable laws of supply and demand; there are a lot of people who want that advertising job, and the advertisers know it. Be willing to start for low pay knowing that as you gain experience, you gain salary.

The bright spot for salaries is the emerging field of Internet advertising. Firms like DoubleClick (see chapter 8) are redefining the way the ad game is played by converging lead generation and fulfillment to the Web. The burgeoning world of Web advertising and e-commerce is injecting new, dynamic growth into a traditional field. Look for huge opportunities in designing, arranging, and selling online advertising.

The large advertising agencies are opening offices all around the world. After years of experience there is a possibility of working on global campaigns. The field of advertising is one of the most global business career options available. The ability to work in a team or to perform individual excellence is important because you will have the opportunity to do both. The advertising and PR fields can result in very satisfying careers. There aren't many jobs which allow your creativity and strategies to come to life to be observed by thousands or even millions of people. Work results are immediate and conspicuous. When you sell yourself, sell the sizzle, but the steak backing it up must be 100 percent prime cut or you're out.

Money Magazine listed the advertising/PR position as one of the fifty best jobs in America. This field has high expected job growth and is part of the rapidly growing service sector. The advertising business is enormous, creating plenty of opportunity for the right person. Last year over $150 billion dollars were spent on advertising and over $160 billion on sales promotion (i.e., coupons, samples, sweepstakes, premiums).

Public relations is directed at the community (the ultimate consumer of the organization), internal employees, stockholders, and other organizations. As a result every organization must perform public relations activities, which means public relations jobs can be found in virtually every industry and organization.

Creative ads are often not the most flashy, but those which address customer needs in a new and direct way. For example, a problem faced by computer network administrators is the daunting task of inventorying every computer in a firm along with serial numbers of components like hard disks and monitors. Compaq recently began an ad campaign aimed directly at these administrators, touting the fact that its new machines performed many of these tasks automatically in the right configuration. It's significant that Compaq was not trying to reach end users of its machines as was traditional among computer hardware marketers.

Advertising and public relations activities can be performed in-house as a part of corporate advertising, or the activities can be conducted by outside agencies. In addition, there are a number of creative houses and support companies that help produce advertising. Jobs in the advertising and public relations fields can be diverse and very challenging.

Traditionally, the fortunes of an ad agency have been driven by the strength of its creative people. Good creativity has meant high profits. This is changing as an agency's prowess in media buying has become increasingly important. In today's world of fragmented media outlets, many advertisers have started to carefully scrutinize the quality of media buys done by their agencies.

A lot of the best work in PR is done in the smaller firms. We have run into our share of stressed press release writers in the big PR firms who spend a lot of time thinking up the next spin for that steel company or trade union. You may find yourself happier and in a position of greater responsibility if you work for a smaller public relations operation.

Agencies which are well-versed in nontraditional media outlets such as the Internet are also gaining new business at a high rate. This trend is likely to continue as the Internet, online services, and home interactive TV grow in size. Now is a good time to combine your marketing savvy with some technical training.

Key Jobs in Advertising and Public Relations

The **Account Executive** is responsible for all aspects of the account. He or she is responsible for understanding the advertising needs of the customer and sharing the needs to other agency personnel. The account executive coordinates the planning, creating, production, and implementation of the campaign.

The **Advertising Media Planner** is responsible for making a series of decisions involved in the delivery of the advertising message to prospective purchasers and users of a product or service. The media planner determines the right mix of television, radio, newspaper, magazine, and other media for the advertising campaign.

The **Copywriter/Artist** category includes all the creative services personnel who write and illustrate the advertising. These individuals write copy, design body copy, design headlines, and draw the ad storyboard, and may become involved with the actual creation of the advertisement.

The **Directors of Advertising/Public Relations** are typically two different people with similar responsibilities for their individual departments. The director is responsible for all advertising or public relations activities except sales. The director will control the entire advertising or public relations campaign including budgeting, planning, coordinating creation, and production of the process. Specific duties will depend on the size of the organization.

The **Media Traffic Manager** analyzes, selects, and contracts for space or time in the various media that will be used in the campaign. The traffic individual must be knowledgeable about the advantages and disadvantages of each of the media and the demographics that they reach. Finally, he or she will make the purchase of the appropriate media and vehicles.

The **Production Manager** is responsible for the physical creation of the ads either in-house or contracted through production houses. The production manager must establish and maintain relations with exterior advertising producers and to ensure the successful completion of the advertisement.

The **Public Relations Specialist** is responsible for determining and evaluating public attitudes and communicating programs designed to bring about public acceptance of an organization. The public relations specialist is much like the advertising account executive. He or she is responsible for managing the public relations of an organization. The public relations specialist may be in-house or a part of an agency.

CORPORATE FINANCE

Supporting every Webmaster and network engineer is a team of business professionals we can lump under the heading, "corporate finance." In many ways, the responsibilities faced by corporate finance types are similar to the challenges of developers and analysts.

Most corporate finance jobs involve solving problems using a combination of intuition and analytics. If you are good at problem solving, this may well be the job area for you. Many of us imagine working in a corporation as a boring, routine experience designed for dim-witted, persnickety pencil-pushers in short-sleeved pastel plaid shirts. Not so. Rather, you need to be comfortable with ambiguity and a rapidly changing environment where tasks change from day to day and sometimes hour to hour.

Corporate finance and the PC are now joined at the hip. To succeed, you have to be computer literate with spreadsheets, word processors, presentation packages, and mainframes in corporate finance. This is especially true for entry-level positions where you will need to crunch numbers as you get involved in the details of corporate financial planning, accounting, and capital raising. When you interview, you'll be asked to expound on grand thoughts about strategy, quality, and vision, but on your first day, you better know how to write a macro in Excel. That's programming, if you didn't know it. You'll also be expected to be able to use a Telerate or Bloomberg workstation.

Movies like *Wall Street* and *Tycoon* portray killer operators in corporate environments getting ahead by manipulation, deceit, and chicanery. This isn't exactly how it works. People who like people, can communicate their ideas, build deep networks, and are passionate about their work get ahead. The number one attribute most corporate employers are looking for is initiative. If you can give examples in interviews of situations where you did something plain useful even though no one asked you to, you will be a hot commodity. Have you ever started a business? Put together a social event that brought people together? Started a new organization?

Large U.S. corporations are more globalized than ever, and jobs will often take you across borders. You will obviously be more desirable to a company if you have a command of at least one foreign language and knowledge of international corporate finance. Would you be comfortable managing a bank relationship for your company in Brazil or costing new plants in Indonesia?

Do you like working with risk? The last decade has seen a dramatic increase in the sophistication of corporate risk management strategies. How are we going to hedge against fluctuations in the cost of our inputs, and what should we do to protect against foreign currency fluctuations? If you are familiar with models, techniques, and derivatives which can be used to manage risk, you will be in high demand.

It is crucial that a financial officer be a team player, whether at the bottom or the top of a company. At the top, relationships are especially important. For a CEO, the chief financial officer is financial whiz, strategist, and partner. The relationship needs to be tight.

While still largely a male world, women are making rapid inroads in corporate finance positions around the United States. According to the *Detroit News*, "Finance has become the first field of opportunity for women because promotions are based on merit—not the old-boy network. Experts say accounting and its natural offspring—finance, treasury, budgeting—are less obstructed by the macho cultures more prevalent in manufacturing and engineering, other traditional paths to the corporate pinnacle."

Corporate finance professionals are increasingly getting involved in value management—the practice of figuring out if shareholder value is being created in each of a company's activities. Look for this practice to get hotter and hotter over time. Some of the most innovative companies in the world are now using value management.

The job of the financial officer is to create value for a company. The four main areas of concentration are liquidity, flexibility, compliance with laws, and regulatory support. The goals of the objective are met through four main activities:

1. designing, implementing, and monitoring financial policies
2. planning and executing the financing program
3. managing cash resources
4. interfacing with the financial community and investors

There is growing interest in integrated methods of risk and liability management. Many companies have decentralized risk management activities where each division or plant can hedge away price and interest-rate risk. Companies are increasingly permitting this but aggregating positions into a book at the corporate level and adding controls.

Many firms are looking for quantitative analysts in their finance group. Merck now employs dozens of rigorous finance professionals who use techniques like neural networks, artificial intelligence, and Monte Carlo simulation to assess new R&D projects. There will be more and more firms who quantitatively make financial and operating choice, for example, choosing a capital structure by balancing off the expected costs and benefits of debt.

A company's finance group is the bridge between the investment community and the shop floor. In a day and age when institutional investors are increasingly active, it's crucial that managers get the message that their job is to create shareholder value. The job of the finance group is to make sure that happens.

A key skill for financial professionals is negotiating ability. Persons who can put the other side at ease at the negotiating table while still getting a good price are invaluable. Many firms are actively engaged in acquisitions strategies and require employees who can evaluate possible partners and then negotiate transactions. Twenty to forty percent of employee costs now come in the form of benefits. Managing benefits cost-effectively has now become a major challenge for financial officers.

Key Jobs in Corporate Finance

Although most of these jobs require considerable experience, they are included here because of how vital they are to any Net organization. A startup will probably have vacancies in some of these areas. If you feel you can add value, start doing the work and build a job around yourself.

Benefits Officer duties involve managing pension fund assets, setting up employee 401(k) plans, determining health care benefits policies, and working with human resources to set up cost-effective employee benefits. This job requires a combination of finance knowledge, knowledge of human resources management, and understanding of organizational behavior.

Cash Manager duties involve establishing relationships with banks, managing short-term credit needs, ensuring that sufficient cash is on hand to meet daily needs, putting excess cash into a concentration account bearing interest, and handling international transfers of funds. This job is detail-oriented and requires good ability to negotiate.

Controller duties involve financial planning, accounting, financial reporting, and cost analysis. This individual will get involved in property, revenue, benefits, derivatives, lease, and joint interest accounting. He or she may need to develop forecasting models to project revenues and costs and may be called on to implement or work with a complex costing system, efforts at financial reengineering, transfer pricing issues, or interface with auditors. This job requires extensive accounting experience. Often holders of this position enter a company from a Big Six accounting firm.

Credit Manager duties include establishing policies for granting credit to suppliers, setting guidelines for collecting on credit, and considering whether to securitize receivables. This job requires knowledge of the customer and ability to analyze accounting statements.

Financial Analyst duties involve determining financing needs, analyzing capital budgeting projects, long-range financial planning, analyzing possible acquisitions and asset sales, visiting credit agencies to explain the firm's position, working on budgets, analyzing competitors, implementing financial plans, monitoring the market price of your firm's securities, analyzing leasing agreements, and determining needs and methods of dealing with derivatives. Often you will be assigned to a specific area, such as revenue planning, capital budgeting, or project finance. This challenging job requires good analytical skills, computer skills, and a broad understanding of finance.

Investor Relations Officer duties involve dealing with the investing public by disseminating financial information, responding to queries from institutional investors, issuing press releases to explain corporate events, and organizing teleconferences with investors. This challenging job involves contacts with top-level executives and requires understanding of finance and public relations. Many who hold this job have backgrounds in PR or advertising.

Real Estate Officer. This job involves finding real estate locations for a company, negotiation of lease agreements, acquisition of real estate, and valuation of properties. This job requires a thorough understanding of finance and real estate.

Treasurer duties involve supervision of the treasury department, which is involved in financial planning, raising funds, cash management, and acquiring and disposing of assets. This is an upper management job that requires both analytical skill and the ability to manage and motivate people.

PRODUCT MANAGEMENT

Product management is one of the most challenging positions within any company. Product managers are responsible for the marketing and development of everything from products and services to experiences. They are responsible for identifying and creating a market segment, positioning the product within the market, and selling the product to customers. They have responsibility for extending market share through a combination of design, marketing, promotion, partnerships, advertising, distribution, and other campaigns.

Product managers are both strategic and tactical. Strategic because they are responsible for positioning a product, assessing the competition, and thinking about the future. Tactical because they are in the field developing appropriate promotional campaigns, talking to reps about what customers want and think, and doing the day-to-day sales tracking that's required for any major product category.

Attributes Required of Product Managers

- Highly analytical thinking
- Sense of ownership and personal responsibility
- Superb communication skills
- Entrepreneurial spirit

The work of a product manager involves positioning a product relative to the competition and consumer interests. They have to assign limited resources to various campaigns; develop a product to keep up with technology, trends, and new ideas; promote a product to make sure that consumers understand its benefits; analyze data on sales of a product in order to understand where it's doing well and where it's not; and monitor the competition to understand what consumers are buying and where the market is going next. Product management professionals are excited about their ability to manage and strengthen brands. They are at the vortex of company life because their decisions directly affect the success of a business, and successful product managers demonstrate several principles of their field:

Analysis is key. Product management is less a people job than many of the other marketing careers. Product management and marketing research require high levels of problem-solving skills and analytical abilities.

Learn to present. As in most marketing careers, presentation skills are a necessity. Both jobs will require presentations to others in the company and for marketing research to clients. The ability to be persuasive will prove to be highly beneficial in building a coalition supporting your position and ideas.

The ultimate marketing job. To many marketing people, a position as product manager is the ultimate marketing job. You are managing the entire marketing operation of a product from inception to final customer distribution.

Experience is imperative. To become a product manager you must obtain years of marketing and selling experience. Most product managers have spent some time in the salesforce. A product manager is not a job that typically goes to someone in their twenties.

A good MBA helps. It is becoming more and more important to obtain a Masters of Business Administration (MBA) degree to become either a product manager or marketing researcher. A masters degree combined with marketing experience is a powerful combination. Schools that are well-known in marketing and product management include Northwestern, Georgetown, Dartmouth, and Ohio State.

Huge international potential. Product management may provide the best opportunity to move into international marketing. Gaining experience on domestic U.S. products provides a great training ground for expanding products internationally. Companies such as Coca-Cola and Unilever are well known for moving people around the world to develop knowledge of specific markets and understanding of product reach and potential.

Fast-track pay scales. Because of the requirements for substantial marketing and selling experience and the growing need for a masters degree, pay for product managers and market researchers can be very high. Many regard product management as the "fast-track" career in the marketing area.

High entry hurdles. It's not surprising then that jobs in product management are more difficult to obtain than other marketing positions. By definition, the number of product manager types is limited by the number of products that generate sufficient revenue to support a full-time product manager.

Key Jobs in Product Management

Assistant Product Manager is the position where most entry-level jobs in the product management category will begin (this may occur after two or more years of selling). The assistant product manager is responsible for various strategic components of the product.

The **Market Analyst** is responsible for researching the market and providing important strategic information to the product managers. The information may come from salespeople, customer research, or databases.

The **Product Category Manager** is responsible for multiple product lines in the product category. They manage multiple product managers and are responsible for the organization's product offerings.

The **Project Director** is responsible for collecting market information on a given marketing or product project. They direct others to gather, analyze, and report market research.

The **Product Manager** has responsibility for several brands within a product line or product group. Some organizations may have brand managers that report to the product manager. The product manager is responsible for developing marketing strategies for the product. The manager also determines extension or deletion of products within the product line.

The **Market Research Director** is responsible for the planning, gathering, and analyzing of all organizational research. Nonindependent agency directors may also be in charge of managing market intelligence, which is everyday market information about the marketing environment.

Salaries and Job Outlook for Product Managers

In general, salaries for product managers and market researchers are relatively high in the U.S. market. Because this category of jobs encourages or requires a masters degree, starting pay will be somewhat higher than other marketing categories. However, some entry-level jobs, particularly in market research, can be low. The following chart lists representative salaries for talented marketing professionals in large corporations in 1998 and 1999.

Product Manager	$60,000–$120,000
Assistant Product Manager	$40,000–$60,000
Product Category Manager	$60,000–$130,000+
Market Analyst	$24,000–$50,000
Project Director	$45,000–$70,000
Market Research Director	$75,000–$140,000

It would be difficult to think of any job that is more in the heart of the company than that of product management. Product managers are the key bridge between the innovators in a corporations and the marketplace. Product managers will always be important and face a great future. At the same time, be ready for failure. Not every product does swimmingly. The key is to experiment by test-marketing new ideas, to understand customers, and to risk losses. Great companies like Coca-Cola have had their share of belly-flops, such as New Coke.

Product management is becoming more and more an international or global concept. The 1990s have seen a dramatic increase in international product management, although much of it may occur locally in international markets. A key strategic decision facing many corporations is whether to integrate their product management efforts.

Computer and statistical skills are vital. Product managers are big-time consumers of research. As a result, they must be good with basic math, statistics, and computer analysis. Problem formulation, data collection, data analysis and interpretation, and communication abilities are skills that will be necessary every day in marketing research.

The world of the product manager is changing with economic growth as well. As the economy grows, there is increasing specialization and competition in each market niche. While this can initially complicate the matter, specialization opens great opportunities to target specific demographic groups. This idea has gained currency in the concept of mass customization, where a company targets products down to the level of the individual. Levi-Strauss, for example, has begun selling blue jeans fit to each individual customer.

Gathering secondary research used to be an arduous task, with hours spent in libraries searching through government documents and other resources. Today the data is much more easily accessed through online databases. The ability to scan information, drill down for detail, and identify relevance is a key skill in the work of today's product manager.

A critical task of any product manager is understanding the receptiveness of customers. Companies such as Guinness (part of brand giant Diageo) have become far more effective in recruiting drinkers by identifying customers as being available (potentially interested in Guinness), sympathetic (drink some Guinness but not yet fanatics), and supporters (enthusiastic about Guinness and willing to ask others to sample the product).

Believe it or not, there is increasing interest in marketers who understand anthropology! Heck, they're even hiring anthropologists. And, why not? These liberal arts majors uncover myths in focus groups and bring an understanding of civilization and culture to product management efforts.

The discipline of marketing is continuing to evolve. The heart of a product manager's job has historically been illustrated by the four Ps, devised in the middle of the 1960s by Harvard Business School professor, N. Borden. The Ps are *product, place, price,* and *promotion*. Today, this basic marketing theory has been challenged to include three other Ps including *people, process,* and *provision* of customer service. Ken Hudson of the Original Thinking Company has suggested instead the five Is: *ideas, imagination, intuition, interruptions,* and *interactions*. Ideas are transformed information with the intention of creating profit. Imagination drives the future of products. "Brand imagination," for example, involves envisioning where a brand could be in five years time and acting today to make the vision happen. Interruptions refer to the need to disrupt familiar patterns of thinking and behaving. Growing market share involves bringing customers around to your way of thinking. Interactions involve the crucial importance of listening and understanding what customers want.

STRATEGIC MARKETING

Strategic marketing has the mission-critical responsibility of positioning the company and driving the 'Selling Chain' concept in the marketplace. Individuals generally specialize in one of the following categories:

Corporate Marketing: Cultivating the corporate image and positioning the company within the company's chosen industry. Also developing relations with leading analysts and the press.

Campaign Management: Organizing major marketing events such as trade shows and seminars, preparing all marketing materials, and directing lead generation activities for the company and its business partners.

Product Marketing: Developing an unmatched understanding of at least one of the company's products or services to determine its specific value proposition and positioning. Also building and maintaining the pipeline of potential purchasers for that product.

Attributes Required of Strategic Marketers

- Strong writing skills

- Excellent presentation skills

- High degree of organization

- Creativity

OTHER KEY BUSINESS CAREERS

Internal Business Consultant

As an integral part of a business unit, internal business consultants are responsible for assessing business and technical project risks, developing explicit plans, managing customer expectations, estimating resources and pricing, and creating proposals for implementation and deployment of solutions to customers. They provide direct project management at the customer site while acting as the interface between the company and the customer's team. Consultants provide technical direction and leadership to clients, extend the company's software to meet clients' requirements, and work closely with the marketing and development teams within their industry business unit.

Most Net companies seek candidates who possess outstanding communication, leadership, and self-management skills. Consultants must develop a comprehensive knowledge of the company's technology and the ability to make implementation decisions based upon an explicit understanding of the technical consequences of those decisions. They also understand and are able to apply the company's process for deployment, and they transfer knowledge of that process to the customer. Consultants must maintain a focus on the impact of the project on the customer's business. Willingness to travel is a necessity. Most Net companies reward the hard work put in by their consultants with lots of responsibility and rich rewards that are linked to outcomes.

Attributes Required of Internal Business Consultants

- Strong technical background

- Programming ability

- Thrive in fast-paced, high-pressure environments

- Professional presence

- Willingness to travel

- Tenacity and aggressiveness

Director of Media Integration

Responsible for managing the life-cycle of a media project. Deals across the spectrum of business functions to integrate everything: 3-D animators, the art department, video graphics production, the Netcast engineers, the sound designers, the executive producers of the shows, the network administrators, the business development people, the software developers, and the president.

Internet Sales Engineer

Serves as the liaison between the customer and sales, engineering, and operations. Handles presales work for Web hosting services, makes recommendations, and makes sure the customer has a smooth implementation. Also works with service line management as a field liaison.

Presales Support

Presales is one of the most challenging positions available in any Net company because it requires a high level of both technical and business aptitudes. Presales individuals are responsible for showing prospective customers how the company's systems and technology can solve the customer's most difficult problems efficiently and elegantly. This process includes presentations, technical reviews, information-gathering sessions, and development of prototype systems using customer-specific information. Presales individuals must thrive in a high-pressure environment and must deliver exceptional performance on both the technical and interpersonal frontiers.

Presales account development is one of the most critical aspects of the sales cycle. This involves technical presentations that establish a level of confidence with the customer, develop an understanding of their products and business model, and determine the proper fit between company technology and the customer's needs. The successful candidate must be able to communicate the benefits of the company's technology to the customer, while keeping the discussion at an appropriate technical level for the audience. For big-ticket software solutions, sales cycles often run into the millions of dollars, requiring the candidate be comfortable and effective in front of everyone from technical experts to CEOs of Fortune 100 organizations. Candidates who enjoy high levels of responsibility are ideal, as presales people have a tremendous amount of account ownership.

Attributes Required of Presales Support

- Great attitude
- Business savvy
- Presentation and teaching skills
- Tenacity
- Aggressiveness
- Inclination to challenge the impossible

To excel in presales support, you must be highly self-motivated, goal- and deadline-oriented, have excellent abstract reasoning ability, and be able to go the extra mile to make your customer successful. Programming experience is expected, and previous experience with configuration and search problems, expert systems, and object-oriented or declarative languages is desirable.

Recruiter

Hiring the best and brightest in the software industry depends on leading human resources practices, resourceful thinking, and outstanding people skills. Working with hiring managers, Microsoft Recruiters determine needs while developing and implementing creative sourcing strategies that involve referral generation, ad placement, position postings, direct sourcing/cold calling, and networking. See chapter 8 for a discussion of a new class of recruiter support called e-searchers.

Recruiter Competencies

- Planning and organizational skills to manage the clients, applicants, and employment processes in a timely and effective manner

- Persuasive skills to sell the applicants on the opportunities for which they are sought and to convince client managers to adopt realistic expectations about finding appropriately qualified candidates in a tight labor market

- Analytical skills to determine and understand the unique requirements for every new job assignment, to research and identify potential sources of new applicants, and to screen candidates against the selection criteria for each position

- The initiative to seek out new and different resources and to go the extra mile with candidates and clients to close the deal

- A healthy dash of good oral and written communications skills, interpersonal skills, energy, and the interest and motivation to be a recruiter

Trainer

Most Net companies have internal trainers, or they outsource the training task to an outside service provider. In either case, the mission of a training group is to educate and continuously inform customers and partners about the technical capabilities of the company's suite of applications as these features relate to their business challenges.

A typical mission statement for a training group also includes an objective to empower the company's customers and partners to be more self-sufficient in customizing and maintaining their applications, while achieving the highest customer satisfaction ranking for training and education in the industry.

Curriculum developers work on producing new courses for existing or recently released products. This role is more focused on assembling information and generating examples and exercises rather than material format and creation. It is expected that curriculum developers can also serve as instructors. They are usually responsible for training the instructors on new courses as well as filling in for other trainers when demand exceeds supply. Curriculum developers receive firsthand experience with the company's applications, architectures, and solutions. They work directly with the product developers to gather information and provide critical feedback for product direction. They develop course outlines and content for partners' certification, customer education, and sales seminars. These individuals are a critical link in ensuring the success of the company's partnerships and implementations.

Attributes Required of Trainers

- Ability to comprehend and convey technical concepts
- Capacity to think quickly on their feet

- Experience with public speaking
- Unwavering patience and universal friendliness

Educators/Trainers

There are many educators and trainers who have jumped on the Net band-wagon. These persons are either training in corporations or teaching in secondary and postsecondary education. There are many titles for Internet educators and trainers. A few are named and described below.

Instructional Designer

Businesses are finding it essential to provide training to their employees in order to remain productive and globally competitive. To provide this training, instructional technologist/designers are usually employed as corporate trainers. Due to the higher availability of information on the Web, these educators are using the Internet and the World Wide Web to teach job-related topics. They are also responsible for developing the training material and course format. In all of their tasks, they use the Internet for creating, editing, and presenting material. The necessary Internet skills include knowledge of how to create a Web site, HTML, basic Internet services such as e-mail and newsgroups, and experience with a Web browser. Other skills would be dependent on the topic being presented. Candidates in this field usually have a degree in Instructional Technology, especially for developing the training material and course format. Companies also employ workers who may have on-the-job expertise and can help in training new hires. These latter trainers have a degree in the technical field for which they generally work.

Net Instructor

Internet instructors usually range from technical school instructors to college professors. They are the persons who have some expertise in the Internet and WWW. They teach all aspects of the Internet and WWW, from HTML/Java/CGI programming to Internetworking technology. They usually teach as a part of a curriculum that leads to the student getting a degree or certificate stating they have completed Net training. The Internet instructor designs, implements, presents, and evaluates course material used for the course. The expected education level covers a wide range of educators and backgrounds. There are the professors who teach undergraduate and graduate courses, and they have M.S. or Ph.D. degrees. There are the pregraduate degree and technical school instructors who have B.S. degrees with extensive experience in Net concepts and usage.

7
Emerging Net Jobs and Skills

It's kind of fun to do the impossible.
—*Walt Disney*

EMERGING NET SKILL REQUIREMENTS

The Internet is creating new jobs all the time just as it is transforming and destroying old ones. Through the tectonic forces it has unleashed, the Internet redefines every job description and profession. At the same time, it is requiring new and ever more specific skill sets. Let's look at the skills required and the emerging jobs that will employ them. First, the skills:

Hot Language Skills

- Visual Basic
- C and C++
- Java
- HTML
- PL/SQL (Oracle)
- XML (Extensible Markup Language)
- Advanced Business Application Programming (SAP report language)

The Hot Networking Skills

- Windows NT
- OpenView (H-P)
- Cisco Works (Cisco Systems)
- Vital Signs (Microsoft System Management Server)
- Internet Protocol
- Extranets
- LAN, WAN
- Frame Relay
- Router, hub, and gateway technology
- Voice-data integration
- Video streaming
- Network design and performance
- Design skills for Fast Ethernet, Gigabit
- Ethernet
- Asynchronous Transfer Mode
- Fiber Distributed Data Interface
- Network Load balancing

The Hot Database Skills

- Data warehousing
- Data mining
- Moving data in and out of SQL-compliant environments
- SQL Server
- Oracle
- Architecture, design, and administration of distributed relational databases
- Object orientation
- Lotus Notes
- Package integration (Baan, SAP, PeopleSoft)
- Visual Basic
- PowerBuilder

Hot Interface Skills

- Human Performance
- Speech Recognition

- Interactivity Design
- Usability
- Meta-Content Development

Hot Business Skills

- Intellectual Property Rights
- Privacy Issues
- Information Security Law
- Knowledge Management
- Mediation

Hot Leadership Skills

- Envisioning: facilitating idea generation and innovation in the team and helping the team members think conceptually and creatively
- Organizing: helping the team focus on details, deadlines, efficiency, and structure so the team gets its work done
- Spanning: maintaining relationships with outside groups and people, networking, and presentation management
- Developing and maintaining a strong team image, intelligence gathering, locating and securing critical team resources
- Socializing: uncovering the needs and concerns of individuals in the group, ensuring that everyone has the opportunity to present his or her views, injecting humor when it is needed to relieve tensions, taking care of the social and psychological needs of group members

MONIKER MANIA

Job titles are really a relic of old, bureaucratic organizations. At one point, they delimited where one job stops and the next one begins. But in today's flattened enterprises, where serving the customer—whatever it takes—has priority over staying within the lines of an organization chart, job titles are just so much extra friction. Job titles were also a cheap way of conferring status. Did people really get satisfaction from a new title instead of a raise? Today, employees say, "Show me the money!" or they're out the door.

But old habits die hard. Everyone thinks they need a job title, and for that reason, everyone does. It's a good thing they are free, which shows how much they are worth. The good news is that a critical mass of Net companies recognizes the essential frivolousness of job titles and has the confidence to play with them. Here is a list of actual job titles held by real people.

- Director of First Impressions
- Chief Energizing Officer
- Web Archaeologist
- Thought Jockey
- Virtual Reality Evangelist
- Senior Freelance Bandit
- Animation Skeptic
- Director, Department of the Future
- Minister of Order and Reason
- Creative Undertaker
- Director of Intelligence
- Manager of Demand Creation
- User Experience Designer
- Site Architect
- Web User Interface Designer
- Content Writer
- Content Software Programmer

EMERGING NET JOBS

Internet Researcher

The Net has radically redefined the art and science of recruitment. One of the emerging opportunities in this area is that of Internet researcher, sometimes known as e-searcher, Internet sourcer, or cyberian. People in these positions serve as resources for recruiters, the people who actually screen and present candidates in response to a client's need to fill a position. They are infomediaries charged with finding the small number of logical resumes or names of potential candidates that the recruiters can then target. The position will draw from the same kinds of people who are attracted to research and detective work.

Most recruiters simply don't have the time to spend hours and hours online searching through millions of resumes and discussion lists for the names of people that can be contacted for a particular opportunity. The skills required of an e-searcher are quite different from those needed to be a recruiter. The two have as much in common as the research librarian and the writer; both complement one another, but rarely are the two skills found in the same person. E-search is a highly skilled process that requires training and experience to become an expert. Most recruiters have neither the technical skill to become good at it nor the personality to spend that kind of time in front of the computer.

E-Search Competencies

- Willingness to spend virtually an entire day on the computer poking around obscure corners of the Net, seeking ways to locate and communicate with potential candidates

- Thorough understanding of Internet search tools and how to use different tools for different searches

- A detective mentality—able to ferret out obscure information

- Skills at helping recruiters more clearly define what they are seeking. A search is only as good as its input. This role of partnering with recruiters and managers to define the job and create the parameters for search will be increasingly important.

- Understanding of advertising and what motivates people to check out the employment section of a corporate Web site. These e-searchers will have to consult with Webmasters and advertising agencies to craft messages that appeal to passive job seekers.

Internet Researchers: In Their Own Words

Because the discipline of e-searching is such a new field, I asked three people actually making a living at it to describe just what it is they do.

First, here is how Kelly Dingee, an Internet sourcer at TTC (*http://www.ttc.com*) describes her responsibilities:

I'm an Internet recruiter/sourcer. My job is to find people via resume databases, job postings and independent searches. I'm extremely fortunate to have worked for my company for five years, the first two as a personnel coordinator, the next two years as a recruiter, and the last year-plus as an Internet recruiter. I've been sourcing on the Internet since 1996, and I now have a part-time opportunity that allows me to source for every position our company has (at 1,200-plus employees, it can be intense). I source VPs and I source accounting assistants. It can be difficult to find engineers, technical sales, and IT types.

I don't screen. I do advise on spending, prepare budget figures, and create Internet recruiting strategies for the five or six full-time recruiters we have on staff. I "manage" all of our Internet recruiting subscriptions and contracts. Since I've been involved in Internet recruiting, I've seen our hires from this source double, and I expect them to more than double this year. My speed at gathering resumes has significantly increased over time. I can now source a little over a thousand on a good month compared to when I started. (These are not ad responses, and I only work 25 hours a week.)

Pat Loomis, a writer/editor/Internet researcher who lives in Redondo Beach (*patloomis@yahoo.com*), reports:

I agree that [e-searching] is a brand new job and a quickly expanding one. I have three clients, and do both research and job posting for them. I fell into this job when I applied for another job with a recruiter and she offered me this job (contract, working from home) when she found out I loved doing research online. From there, I've managed to expand the business by finding other firms who'd like to use my services. It helps that I live in Southern California where there are so many recruiting firms.

If you do a search on Headhunter.net, you'll find many recruiters looking for a researcher (also called a resourcer, sourcer, or cybrarian). I've talked to a number of recruiters, and most of them like the idea, although some are not ready to change the way they've been working and use a researcher. I also help large recruiting firms that have research departments.

Before you go into this field, make sure you'd be right for the job. Are you the kind of person who can sit in front of a computer for hours, searching for something? Patience, obviously, is very important! Some people need to be doing ten things at once—they enjoy multi-tasking. They probably would not be right for the job of Internet researcher. It's takes a focused attention to do the job right. Do not assume that because you can "surf" the Net, you're perfect for this job! You need enough of an administrative background (i.e., a professional awareness) to be able to interact with recruiters as well as potential clients. You'll be representing your client and need to do that in a polished, professional manner. This includes proper English, especially in e-mails.

Next, we hear from David Howard, Systems Administrator, at Messina Management Systems (*http://www.messinamgmt.com*):

I am an Internet researcher, although we title it "Internet recruiter." I am also our systems administrator. The things I research are potential online partnerships (i.e., banner swaps and such), search engine placement, headhunter/resume sites, jobs postings (as well as Webmaster of our own site search for individual resumes using Boolean searches with the various engines). I also do "special requests" so that if a recruiter needs a specific type of person, I try to target that one type of person. I do not, however, contact any of the candidates. That is for the recruiter to do, just as they would anyway. I find them, prescreen them for some basic criteria, and then forward them to the appropriate recruiter.

Finally, Christa Kennis, Project Coordinator, Management Recruiters International (*ckk@mricols.com*) talks about her ambitions in this area:

I have been trying to network with Internet researchers myself. I have been considering becoming an Internet researcher with my current company (a third party search firm). I am currently a recruiter and want to incorporate the research aspect into my position (I worked for a public library system for twelve years, so the digging and researching is rather ingrained). Some of the tasks and projects that I would do as an Internet researcher would be to prepare a call list of companies for a specific job order, gather information on organizations and associations to target, search for leads on potential job orders, visit corporate sites to name gather, post jobs, and search for resumes on job boards. These are the more obvious things that I would do, and we're still working on other duties or special requests that our recruiters may have. I'd love to hear what some of the other Internet researchers have to say regarding their positions. We are still working out the specifics duties and compensation.

Sensory Interface Developer

The biggest area for progress in the next few years may well be in interface design. If so, the sensory interface developer will be on the leading edge. The goal of this job is to eliminate the seams between computers and the humans who use them. We will be seeing entirely new ways to allow a computer to recognize what the user wants and deliver more useful feedback.

E-Business Evangelist

It is unrealistic to think that just because an organization starts on the road to e-business, all the business units will go along willingly. They won't. Some will take a wait-and-see attitude. Others will offer more active resistance. Until they are shown what's in it for them, they will do business as usual. The job of the e-business evangelist is to demonstrate the compelling benefits of getting with the program. Companies such as Cisco have teams of these people internally promoting Cisco's new initiatives.

Subject Matter Mentor

Enterprises demand "just-in-time" learning customized to their environments. Subject matter mentors provide the content and infrastructure for this service, in which knowledge can be "tiered" and delivered on a customized basis.

Niche Mediators

The transition from a suspicious, competitive workplace that hoards knowledge to a cooperative, seamless organization in which knowledge is shared won't be easy. Enter niche mediators whose goal it is to resolve disputes in a nonconfrontational, win-win manner.

PART 3
Internet Job Resources

The best way to predict the future is to create it.

—*Peter Drucker*

YOU HAVE WON THE WAR

Since time immemorial, bosses have had the power. As long as capital was the most important consideration in creating jobs, the golden rule applied: Those who have the gold make the rules. But guess what? In the Net Economy at least, capital is no longer the most important driver of creating value. Talent is. And in Silicon Valleys all over the world, the war for talent is over. You've won. This massive shift in power puts you in the driver's seat, figuratively and perhaps literally. In a desperate desire to recruit and retain the best talent, a number of firms are leasing cars for all their employees.

Whatever your father or even older brother told you about recruiting is not only wrong but irrelevant. Having won the war, you, the applicant, get to demand almost anything and maybe even get it. Top performers, IT people, and experienced managers are now in the driver's seat. Recruiters recognize the shift in power and are changing the way they recruit to fit this new reality. Some implications:

Your value goes up daily. In the traditional economy, companies could use a yearly salary survey to determine the market value of candidates. In the new reality, your economic values change on an almost daily basis. Easily accessible Web page salary surveys and e-mails between friends and with headhunters now means candidates know their market value. Perfect salary information means that companies can no longer fool the applicants with a weak monetary offer. Just like the dealer's price on new cars, the Net Economy means that candidate value is no longer a secret.

Speed is everything. Top firms have found that the 10/10 rule works: the top 10 percent of the candidates accept jobs within 10 days. That means the end of indecisive managers and slow HR administration. Increasingly you will find that companies have a one-day interview and offer process for key positions. Occasionally, by prequalifying you, employers will be able to give you an offer letter before you leave the interview site.

Auction your services. As we get used to the idea of bidding for rental cars, airplane tickets, hotels, and other services, get ready for the idea of putting your services out for bid. Given the multiple offers that many of you will get, that's essentially what's happening, anyway.

In the concluding section of *Internet Jobs!* you will find some resources to help guide you in your quest for a Net job.

THE ONE HUNDRED HOTTEST COMPANIES ON THE NET

Chapter 8 lists the top 100 companies on the Net. Like any such list, this one is based on some more or less arbitrary criteria having to do with growth, innovation, scope, and prospects for success. All of these companies are hiring for the types of positions described in this book. Things change so rapidly in the Net Economy that it's possible that by the time you read this, merger and acquisition activity will have eliminated some names. That's just more evidence that events move very quickly in the Net Economy, and if you're not agile, you will be left behind.

If you believe I made glaring and unforgivable errors of commission or omission in compiling this list, let me save you the trouble of arguing with me. I agree with you. Ultimately, like the list of the top 100 movies of all time, a list like this is a judgment call that reveals more about the list maker than anything else. Nevertheless, I hope you will find the list useful as a resource in your research and job hunting process. Remember, the Web site at *www.jkador.com/netjobs* provides updates and hotlinks to all these companies plus other resources.

8

The One Hundred Hottest Companies on the Net

The one hundred hottest Net companies, in alphabetical order, are:

1. 3Com
2. Active Software
3. ALLTEL
4. Amazon.com
5. Amdahl Corporation
6. America Online
7. Ameritech
8. Andersen Consulting
9. Apple Computer
10. Ascend
11. AT&T
12. Bell Atlantic
13. Bloomberg Financial
14. BMC Software, Inc.
15. Broad Vision, Inc.
16. Cablevision Systems, Inc.
17. CheckFree Corporation
18. Cisco Systems
19. Compaq Computer
20. Computer Associates International
21. DataChannel, Inc.
22. Data General
23. Dell Computer
24. The Walt Disney Company
25. DoubleClick
26. E*TRADE
27. Earthlink Network
28. eBay
29. Electronic Arts
30. Electronic Data Systems
31. Epicor Software
32. Excite@Home
33. Exodus Communications
34. FileNET Corporation

35. Fore Systems, Inc.
36. Gateway Computer
37. Gemplus
38. GTE Corporation
39. Hewlett-Packard
40. IBM
41. Informix Software, Inc.
42. Infoseek
43. Infospace, Inc.
44. Inktomi
45. Intel
46. Intermedia
47. Interwoven
48. Intuit
49. Lawson Software
50. Level 3 Communications
51. Lucent Technologies
52. MCI WorldCom
53. Micron Technology
54. Microsoft
55. MindSpring Enterprises
56. Moai Technologies, Inc.
57. NCR
58. Netcom Systems
59. Netscape Computer Corporation
60. Network Associates
61. Newbridge Networks
62. Nortel Networks Corporation
63. Novell
64. Open Market, Inc.
65. Oracle
66. PairGain Technologies
67. Paradyne
68. Phone.Com
69. Pitney Bowes
70. Pixar
71. QLogic
72. QUALCOMM
73. Qwest Communications International, Inc.
74. RealNetworks
75. Remedy Corporation
76. Renaissance Worldwide
77. SAP AG
78. SAS Institute
79. SBC Communications
80. The Charles Schwab Corporation
81. Science Applications International (SAIC)
82. Siebel Systems, Inc.
83. Silicon Graphics, Inc.
84. Sprint
85. Sun Microsystems
86. Sybase
87. Symbian
88. Telcordia
89. Tellabs
90. Texas Instruments
91. Time Warner
92. Trend Micro, Inc.
93. Trilogy Software
94. U S WEST
95. Vantive Corp.
96. Visual Networks
97. Vitria Technology, Inc.
98. Whistle Communications
99. Xylan Corporation
100. Yahoo!

As information about companies and their recruiting situation changes hourly, it makes little sense to get too granular in a book such as this. The reader will find dynamic links to all these companies and their recruiting Web sites, if they have one, at *www.jkador.com/netjobs*.

3Com

www.3com.com
CEO Eric A. Benhamou
Employees 13,500
Tel: 408-764-5000
Fax: 408-764-5001
Santa Clara, CA

3Com, from "computer, communication, and connectivity," is the world's number-two maker of computer networking products (after Cisco Systems). It develops, manufactures, and supports information access products and networking systems that, locally and globally, connect people to one another. These systems provide access to the wealth of textual, audio, and visual information that has become a vital part of business, education, and entertainment. 3Com provides customers with all the elements required to build a solid networking infrastructure from a single source.

Active Software

www.activesw.com
CEO R. James Green
Employees 102
Tel: 408-988-0414
Fax: 408-988-6607
Santa Clara, CA

Active Software develops products that help customers integrate disparate information resources across the Internet, Intranet, and Extranet. The ActiveWeb Integration System is a suite of software products that is simple, flexible, scaleable, and manageable. Nearly 80 percent of Active Software's sales are from product licensing, consulting, and maintenance. Training accounts for the rest. ActiveWeb provides the broadest range of connectivity and integration in the industry.
Contact:

Active Software
3333 Octavius Drive
Santa Clara, CA 95054
E-mail: hr@activesw.com
Phone: (408) 988-0414
Fax: (408) 988-6607

ALLTEL

www.alltel.com
CEO Joe T. Ford
Employees 21,504
Tel: 408-996-1010
Fax: 408-996-0275
Little Rock, AK

ALLTEL can structure a technology solution based on individual situations from a single software application to full information technology outsourcing, It is a customer-focused information technology company that provides wireline and wireless communications and information services. ALLTEL's communications businesses provide local telephone, long distance, and wireless services to 2.7 million customers in fourteen states, while ALLTEL's information services operations provide information processing, software, and services to financial and telecommunications clients in forty-eight countries. (ALLTEL's wireless business nearly quadrupled with the

1998 purchase of 360 Communications.) In addition, ALLTEL operates a directory publishing company and a communications and data equipment supply business.

Amazon.com

www.amazon.com
CEO Jeffrey P. Bezos
Employees 2,100
Phone: 206-622-2335
Fax: 206-622-2405
Seattle, WA

Billed as "Earth's biggest book and music store," Amazon.com has proved to be one of the brightest spots in the fast-evolving field of business-to-consumer e-commerce. In addition to beating out stealthy book seller-competitors, Amazon.com reports some of the highest visitor numbers of all commerce sites. Amazon's online catalogue allows visitors to search for books by author, title, subject, or keyword. Dealing directly with distributors and publishers, Amazon.com offers discounts of up to 40 percent.

Contact:

Strategic Growth
Amazon.com
P.O. Box 80185
Seattle, WA 98108-0185

Be sure to mention the position and job number for which you are applying. Note that any writing samples you submit along with your resume will not be returned. After you apply: You will receive an acknowledgment, and, if applicable, they will search for a match between the data you have provided and existing openings. FYI: reference checking is extremely thorough.

Amdahl Corporation

www.amdahl.com
CEO David B. Wright
Employees 13,000
Phone: 408-746-6000
Fax: 408-773-0833
Toll Free: 800-538-8460
Sunnyvale, CA

A subsidiary of Japan's Fujitsu (which manufactures most of Amdahl's hardware), Amdahl Corporation provides integrated computing solutions. The Amdahl portfolio includes hardware, software, tools, and operational and consulting services that offer customers a choice in creating powerful technology-based information enterprises.

Amdahl uses optical scanning technology. When mailing your resume, be sure you use a 12-point font with minimal use of bullets, italics, underlining and holding.

Mail to:

Amdahl Corporation
Staffing Department-M/S 300
Attn: WWW
1250 East Arques Avenue
P.O. Box 3470
Sunnyvale, CA 94088-3470
E-mail: (ASCII Text) jobs@amdahl.com

America Online

www.aol.com
CEO Stephen M. Case
Employees 8,500 (US)
Tel: 703-448-8700
Fax: 703-265-2039
Dulles, VA

America Online, Inc., is a provider of interactive communications and services with over $1.6 billion in revenue during fiscal 1997. America Online offers its online services in the United States, Austria, Canada, France, Germany, Japan, Sweden, Switzerland, and the United Kingdom and offers access to its AOL service in more than 100 countries. America Online, Inc., operates three product groups: AOL Interactive Services, AOL Channel Line-Up, Instant Messages, and full Internet services.

Ameritech

www.ameritech.com
CEO Richard Notebaert
Employees 74,000
Phone: 312-750-5000
Fax: 312-207-0016
Chicago, IL

Ameritech, which fellow Baby Bell SBC Communications is buying, offers cellular, long distance, paging, cable TV, security monitoring, electronic commerce, managed services, and wireless data communications for much of the United States and many parts of Europe. It also provides Security Link security-monitoring services to more than one million customers and has teamed with Walt Disney, SBC, and phone companies BellSouth and GTE to deliver video programming.
Contact:

Custom Business Services
Attn: ABINHOMG
225 W. Randolph–23B
Chicago, IL 60606
Fax: (419) 422-6637, Attn: ABINHOMG

Andersen Consulting

www.ac.com
CEO George T. Shaheen
Employees 62,000
Phone: 312-693-0161
Fax: 312-693-7643
Chicago, IL

Andersen Consulting is the world's largest management consulting firm. With multinational clients in a wide range of industries, Andersen maintains offices from Atlanta to Zurich. Whatever a company might do, Andersen Consulting can tell it how the company can do it better and faster with cutting-edge technology and training. The company's success stems from its global presence and technical competence; it trains its professional staff intensively and works directly with major computer and software suppliers. After years of discord, the firm is attempting to break away from its parent, Andersen Worldwide, one of the Big Five accounting firms.

Apple Computer

www.apple.com
CEO Steve Jobs
Employees 9,311
Tel: 408-996-1010
Fax: 408-996-0275
Cupertino, CA

Founded in 1976 by Steve Jobs, Apple makes the Macintosh computer and the MacOS operating system. Its other products include peripherals, laptops, handheld devices, servers, Internet tools, and networking and connectivity products.

Ascend

www.ascend.com
CEO Mory Ejabat
Employees 721
Phone: 510-769-6001
Fax: 510-747-2300
Alameda, CA

Ascend Communications is a provider of technology and equipment solutions for telecommunications carriers, Internet service providers, and corporate customers worldwide. Ascend delivers a set of solutions in the key areas required to build a public and private network infrastructure from end to end. Today the majority of the leading international Post and Telephone companies, global carriers, and network service providers offer Internet access using Ascend equipment. Ascend has installed more than 3.5 million access concentrator ports at ISP, carrier, and corporate enterprise sites throughout the world.

AT&T

www.att.com
CEO C. M. Armstrong
Employees 130,000
Tel: 212-387-5400
Fax: 212-387-5965
New York, NY

Founded in 1885, AT&T is a global company that provides a full menu of communications and information services. AT&T offers customers as little or as much as they want in whatever combinations—or "bundles"— they want. At the same time, AT&T remains committed to providing its traditional voice, data, and video services to businesses and consumers.

Contact:

AT&T Resume Scanning Center
1200 Peachtree Street
Promenade 1
Room 7061
Atlanta, GA 30309-3579
E-mail: work @att.com
Plain text only

Bell Atlantic

www.bellatlantic.com
CEO Ivan G. Seidenberg
Employees 141,000
Tel: 212-395-2121
Fax: 212-395-1285
New York, NY

Providing local telephone service to 26 million customers in 13 northeastern states and Washington, D.C., Bell Atlantic offers cellular, consumer marketing, directory management, Internet access, long distance, wireless, and calling card services, among others. It became a $29 billion company with its 1997 purchase of fellow Baby Bell NYNEX. The company also has telecommunications investments in Greece, Indonesia, Italy, Mexico, New Zealand, Poland, Thailand, the United Kingdom, and other countries. The NYNEX acquisition, the second largest in U.S. history (behind RJR Nabisco's buyout) made Bell Atlantic the number-two U.S. phone company, after AT&T.

Bell Atlantic conducts its recruiting process in a decentralized manner; each Human Resources department has its own application procedures and requirements. Check out the employment Web page to get the best idea of the process at www.bel-atl.com/jobpost. For associate positions, Bell Atlantic has set up telephone hotlines by region, such as New York City (800-511-8086), New England (800-

510-2595), and Pennsylvania (800-678-4869). Resumes for these jobs should be sent with your Social Security number to:

Bell Atlantic Recruitment
P.O. Box 1454
Melville, NY 11747

Nonmanagement and technical positions are also available; call (800) 617-JOBS for up-to-the-minute postings. Bell Atlantic also recruits heavily on college campuses.

Bloomberg Financial

www.bloomberg.com
CEO Michael Bloomberg
Employees 4,000
Tel: 212-318-2000
Fax: 212-980-4585
New York, NY

Bloomberg Financial is an online information service offering a worldwide customer base of corporations, issuers, financial intermediaries, and institutional investors. Bloomberg also produces related media products for distribution in the United States, Canada, Europe, the Middle East, Latin America, Australia, and Asia. In April 1998, Bloomberg agreed to a three-year partnership with America Online. Bloomberg becomes an anchor tenant in AOL's Business News Center and will provide other areas of the site with news coverage.

BMC Software, Inc.

www.bmc.com
CEO Max P. Watson Jr.
Employees 2,777
Tel: 713-918-8800
Fax: 713-918-8000
Houston, TX

BMC Software, Inc., is a worldwide developer and vendor of Cooperative Enterprise Management Solutions that improve the management of business-critical applications and data, as well as optimize the performance of that critical data in complex computing environments. With a 1999 purchase of rival software maker Boole & Babbage, BMC continues to expand its product list through partnerships and acquisitions.

Broad Vision, Inc.

www.broadvision.com
CEO Pehong Chen
Employees 188
Tel: 650-261-5100
Fax: 650-261-5900
Redwood City, CA

Broad Vision, Inc., develops and markets software solutions for dynamic, personalized, one-to-one Web site applications. The company's highly adaptable One-to-One solutions are simply integrated with existing enterprise systems, allowing companies quick and painless establishment on the Web. The company's target customers are Global 1000 businesses, Web content providers, systems integrators, Web developers, and software VARs that are engaged in developing and operating personalized Web sites for consumers, business partners, and employees in electronic commerce, customer support, and interactive content publishing.

Resumes and cover letters may be posted to:

Broad Vision
Att: Human Resources
585 Broadway
Redwood City, CA 94063
Fax: 650-261-5900
E-mail: hr@broadvision.com

Cablevision Systems, Inc.

www.cablevision.com
CEO William Bell
Employees 15,020
Phone: 516-364-8450
Fax: 516-393-1780
Woodbury, NY 11797

The nation's sixth largest operator of cable television systems, Cablevision Systems, Inc., is headquartered in Woodbury, New York. The company serves 2.8 million cable television customers in nineteen states, with major operations clustered in Boston, Cleveland, and New York. Cablevision owns cable channels (American Movie Classics, Bravo, The Independent Film Channel, and MuchMusic). Its Long Island system serves more than 660,000 customers and is the second largest single cable television system in the United States.

Contact:

Cablevision, Corporate Staffing and
    Recruitment
1111 Stewart Avenue
Bethpage, NY 11714
Fax: (516) 803-3134
E-mail: isjobs@cablevision.com

CheckFree Corporation

www.checkfree.com
CEO Peter J. Knight
Employees 1,200
Tel: 770-441-3387
Norcross, GA

CheckFree Corporation is a provider of electronic commerce processing services and software products for more than 850 financial institutions, 1.8 million consumers, and 1,000 businesses. CheckFree designs, develops, and markets services that enable its customers to make electronic payments and collections, automate paper-based recurring financial transactions, and conduct secure transactions on the Internet. Through its processing engine, CheckFree provides financial institutions and their business and consumer customers with unrestricted access, choice, and control. CheckFree means home banking, bill payment, and Web investing through any channel, including touch-tone phones, personal computers, and the World Wide Web.

Cisco Systems

www.cisco.com
CEO John Chambers
Employees 13,650
Tel: 408-526-4000
    or 800-533-6387
Fax: 408-526-4100
San Jose, CA
Cupertino, CA

Cisco Systems is a provider of networking for the Internet. Cisco's networking solutions connect people, computing devices, and computer networks, allowing people to access or transfer information without regard to differences in time, place, or type of computer system.

Cisco provides end-to-end networking solutions that publics use to build a unified information infrastructure of their own or to connect to someone else's network. An end-to-end networking solution is one that provides a common architecture that delivers consistent network services to all users. The broader the range of network services, the more capabilities a network can provide to users connected to it.

Compaq Computer

www.compaq.com
Chairman: Ben Rosen
Employees 71,000 (US)
Tel: 281-370-0670
Fax: 281-514-2656
Houston, TX 77070

Compaq Computer is the number-one PC maker in the world and the third-largest computer seller, behind IBM and Hewlett-Packard. Compaq products are sold and supported in more than 100 countries through a network of authorized Compaq marketing partners. Compaq Computer Corporation designs, develops, manufactures and markets a wide range of computing products, including desktop computers, portable computers, workstations, communications products, and tower PC servers and peripheral products that store and manage data in network environments. Compaq markets its products primarily to business, home, government, and education customers, operating in one principal industry segment across geographically diverse markets.

Compaq accepts resumes through both e-mail and regular mail. Applicants should consult the company's career Web page, located at www.compaq.com/jobs. You may e-mail your resume to Compaq at careerpaq @compaq.com. Plain ASCII text, please.

Computer Associates International

www.cai.com
CEO Charles Wang
Employees 17,500
Tel: 516-342-5224
Fax: 516-342-5734
Islandia, NY

Computer Associates International, Inc., is an example of a mature information technology company that has in the last few years become almost totally Web-enabled. Founded in 1976, CA made its mark by assembling through development and acquisition a world-class portfolio of software systems. CA is the world leader in mission-critical business software. The company develops, licenses, and supports more than 500 integrated products that include enterprise computing and information management, application development, manufacturing, and financial applications. CA makes more kinds of software for more kinds of computers than any other company in the world.

More recently, the Islandia, New York–based company has integrated its efforts around a few core products, all of which exploit the benefits of the Net. At the same time, CA, which has always had a relatively flat and nonbureaucratic operating structure, has used the Net to further streamline its processes and drive autonomy to the points closest to the customer. In everything it does, CA is committed to using technology, including the Net, to better serve its customers by aligning IT with strategic business goals. This commitment to serving customers has paid off. CA is currently the second largest independent software company (next to Microsoft), with 1998 revenues of $5.3 billion. CA employs more than 17,500 people at 160 offices in 43 countries.

For most of its twenty-five-year existence, CA has served its customers in the fashion of all technology companies. CA put its efforts into figuring out how its customers could use computers to work smarter, save time, and reduce costs. This was important work, and with its hundreds of applications and systems software products, CA did it better than anyone. More recently, CA's Chairman and CEO, Charles B. Wang, has committed

CA's efforts in a new, more powerful direction. "No longer will IT serve the bottom line alone," Wang declares. "In today's world that's not good enough. Today, IT must serve the top line by enabling customers to create new opportunities, find markets that did not exist before, exploit new channels, and leverage new partners." To this end, CA is committed to making systematic use of the Internet, both for its development efforts, its internal processes, and to present CA to the world.

For many years, CA has been recognized by magazines as diverse as *Fortune* and *Computerworld* as one of the most desirable places in the world to work. One of the foremost reasons for this recognition is CA's commitment to training and development programs. This aggressive training regimen not only keeps employees up-to-date on the latest skills, it facilitates one of the fastest career advancement tracks in the industry.

To bring out the best in every employee, CA spends millions annually on training and development programs. The company offers virtually continuous rounds of technical workshops and developer seminars worldwide with generous tuition-reimbursement programs. CA views this as an investment in the future—for its employees, and the company.

You can apply online by submitting your resume using an easy online form.

E-mail your resume in ASCII text to:
resumes-usa-r1@cai.com
Call the Islandia, New York, office at:
(800) 454-3788
Mail your resume to:
Human Resources Dept./NET
Computer Associates International, Inc.
One Computer Associates Plaza
Islandia, NY 11749

DataChannel, Inc.

www.datachannel.com
CEO Dave Pool
Employees 50
Tel: 425-462-1999
Fax: 425-637-1192
Bellevue, WA

DataChannel focuses on development of active content technologies, an emerging class of applications that use XML (Extensible Markup Language) to deliver active content to all levels of networked computing (desktop, server, Internet, Intranet, Extranet, VPNs, LANS, WANs).

DataChannel requests that you e-mail your resume to:

hr@datachannel.com

Data General

www.dg.com
CEO Ronald L. Skates
Employees 4,700
Tel: 508-898-5000
Fax: 508-836-4209
Westborough, MA

Data General Corporation is an open systems company specializing in servers, storage products, and services for information systems users worldwide. Data General's range of products and services includes database servers, communications and networking servers, workstations, desktop and portable systems, mass storage subsystems based on open computing technology, thousands of application solutions offered in conjunction with various third-party firms, and a worldwide service and support network. Data General and its subsidiaries, distributors and representatives serve customers in more than seventy countries.

E-mail: resumes@dg.com
For college/intern/co-op:
   newgrads@dg.com.

Include the word *resume* in the subject field of your e-mail. Be sure to indicate the position code (listed beside the position title). Send ASCII text files only. You can apply online using their Web site form.

Mail to:

Data General Corporation
Corporate Staffing
4400 Computer Drive, MSE110
Westboro, MA 01580
Fax: (508) 898-4686

European Applications—

E-mail: Human Resources Europe. Include the word *c.v.* followed by "www.dg.com" in the subject field of your e-mail. Be sure to indicate the position code (listed beside the position title). Send ASCII text files only.

Fax: +44 (0) 181 758 6951
Mail to:

Data General Europe, Data General Tower
Great West Road
Brentford TW8 9AN
Middlesex
United Kingdom

Dell Computer

www.dell.com
CEO Michael S. Dell
Employees 16,000
Phone: 512-338-4400
Fax: 512-728-3653
Round Rock, TX

Dell Computer is one of the world's top PC makers and the world's number-one direct-sale computer vendor. Led by founder Michael Dell (the longest-tenured CEO of any major U.S. computer company), who owns 14 percent of his creation, the company sells hardware and markets third-party software and peripherals. Products include notebooks, PCs, and network servers.

The Walt Disney Company

www.disney.com
CEO Michael D. Eisner
Employees 117,000
Phone: 818-560-1000
Fax: 818-560-1930
Burbank, CA

The world's number-two media company (behind Time Warner), Disney has interests in TV and movie production (including Buena Vista Motion Pictures Group, Buena Vista Television, and Miramax Films), theme parks (including Animal Kingdom, Disneyland, Disneyland Paris, Tokyo Disneyland, Disney-MGM Studios, Epcot Center, and North America's most-visited theme park, the Magic Kingdom in Orlando, Florida), publishing companies, a cruise line, Internet companies (Infoseek), and professional sports franchises (the Anaheim Mighty Ducks of the NHL). The division ABC, Inc., includes the ABC-TV network, nearly a dozen TV stations, and shares in nine cable channels, including sportscaster ESPN.

DoubleClick

www.doubleclick.net
CEO Kevin O'Connor
Employees 700 (US)
Tel: 212-683-0001
Fax: 212-889-0062
New York, NY

Named by *Fortune* magazine one of the "Hip, Hot and Happening Companies" of the year not long after DoubleClick began in 1996, the company's online banner-ads reached 10 million users in just five months. DoubleClick is an Internet advertising network that builds online, one-to-one relationships between brands and consumers and is an advertising network for the World Wide Web. It offers advertisers the ability to distribute their ad banners to multiple sites, representing a full range of users, including investors, business professionals, college students, women, consumers, gamers, and sports enthusiasts. DoubleClick customizes advertising messages to the users who are most appropriate for their products and services through an advanced proprietary targeting technology.

Go to DoubleClick's Web site employment page at www.doubleclick.net. Resumes and cover letters may be e-mailed to specific contacts mentioned in the job descriptions.

E*TRADE

www.etrade.com
CEO Christos Cotsakos
Employees 833
Phone: 650-842-2500
Fax: 650-842-8681
Palo Alto, CA

The number-three online brokerage firm (Charles Schwab is number one) lets its almost 550,000 account holders trade stock through online services, the Internet (about 80 percent of trading volume), and by phone. Leading a new breed of cyber-brokers, E*TRADE can make just about anyone a stock market player as long as they have a computer and a desire to learn.

E*TRADE also offers market data, cash and portfolio management services, and options trading. Through joint ventures the company also operates in such countries as Canada, France, Germany, Japan, the Netherlands, and Poland. SOFTBANK, their joint ventures partner in E*TRADE Japan, owns 28 percent of the company. E*TRADE is buying TeleBanc, an Internet-based bank.

Visit the "Job Opportunities" section of E*TRADE's Web site for details on openings. Resumes and cover letters may be forwarded via fax, e-mail, or regular post to the human resources contact at each office.

Earthlink Network

www.earthlink.net
CEO C. G. "Garry" Betty
Employees 1,343
Phone: 626-296-2400
Fax: 626-296-2470
Pasadena, CA
Cupertino, CA

Unlike other Internet service providers, Earthlink's only focus is on serving the customer. Earthlink Network has more than one million customers throughout the United States and Canada. It vies with MindSpring for the number-four spot among U.S. ISPs (behind America Online, the Microsoft Network, and AT&T World-Net). Sprint owns 29.5 percent of EarthLink; EarthLink's services are co-branded as EarthLink Sprint Internet.

You can send cover letters and resumes via e-mail, fax, or post them (include salary requirements) to Michael Ihde at:

Earthlink Network
3100 New York Dr.
Pasadena, CA 91107

You can also fax your resume at (408) 974-5691

eBay

www.ebay.com
CEO Margaret Whitman
Employees 500
Phone: 408-558-7400
Fax: 408-558-7401
San Jose, CA

eBay is a person-to-person Internet trading community in which users buy and sell personal items in an auction format. If an item sells, eBay will charge the seller a percentage of the closing price. The company has extended its reach in the auction industry by acquiring Butterfield & Butterfield, the number-three auction house in the United States.

E-mail resumes to the Staffing Department at jobs@ebay.com (ASCII text only format).

Mail to:

eBay, Inc.
2005 Hamilton Ave., Suite 350
San Jose, CA 95125
Fax: (408) 369-4839.
FYI: E-mailed resumes preferred

Electronic Arts

www.ea.com
CEO Lawrence Probst III
Employees 2,100
Phone: 650-628-1500
Fax: 650-628-1413
Redwood City, CA

Electronic Arts (EA) is a leading computer game maker. Almost half of EA's sales come from outside the United States, and the company has distribution centers in more than seventy-five countries. The San Mateo, California-based entertainment software giant operates like a movie studio, with producers coordinating the work of artists, writers, animators, sound engineers, musicians, set designers, and programmers. Under different brand names (including EA Sports and Jane's Combat Simulations), the company publishes nearly 100 games, such as *Madden NFL* and *SimCity*.

Sign up with their online recruitment system at www.ea-recruiter. If you'd prefer, simply e-mail them at: jobs@ea.com.

Resumes can be sent via U.S. Mail to:

Electronic Arts
P.O. BOX 9025
Redwood City, CA 94065-9025
Fax: (650) 628-5900

Electronic Data Systems

www.eds.com
CEO Jeffrey M. Heller
Employees 120,000
Phone: 972-604-6000
Fax: 972-605-2643
Plano, TX

Founded by Texas billionaire and presidential candidate Ross Perot (now head of rival Perot Systems), Electronic Data Systems (EDS) is the largest independent systems consulting company in the United States (IBM is number one). EDS offers corporate outsourcing, data center management, online consulting, and reengineering for businesses and governments. EDS, which also provides management consulting services through subsidiary A. T. Kearney, was spun off by General Motors (GM) in 1996; about a fourth of its sales still come from GM contracts and affiliates. In a heavy-duty alliance with MCI WorldCom, EDS is swapping assets, employees, and services with MCI and has acquired its information technology services firm, MCI Systemhouse.

EDS accepts resumes for most entry-level positions on a continuing basis. Applicants should fax their resumes to (972) 605-2643, with cover letters that detail their career interests and geographical preferences, or e-mail their resume to staffing@eds.edu.

Epicor Software

www.epicor.com
CEO L. George Klaus
Employees 624
Phone: 949-453-4000
Fax: 949-453-4091
Irvine, CA

Simply put, Epicor Software helps companies manage their money. The company (formerly Platinum Software) develops enterprise resource planning software products that help businesses handle everything from payables and receivables to inventories, budgets, purchasing, distribution, and foreign currency transactions. Subsidiary DataWorks makes manufacturing management software. Focusing on midsize firms and divisions of large companies, Epicor's customers include financial, insurance, education, hospitality, and technology firms. The company generates more than 70 percent of its sales in the United States and sells its software primarily through telesales and resellers.

Resumes may be faxed to (949) 453-4091
Mail to:

Human Resources Department,
    attention Nancy Orr

195 Technology Dr.
Irvine, CA 92618-2402
E-mail resumes to: www.epicor.com

Excite@Home

www.home.net
CEO Thomas Jermoluk
Employees 570
Phone: 650-569-5000
Fax: 650-569-5100
Redwood City, CA

Formed when @Home bought Excite, Excite@Home uses cable TV systems to provide high-speed Internet access to consumers (@Home) and businesses (@Work) and operates the Excite Internet portal. The company is a member of the new breed of Internet service providers that wants to bring high-speed Internet users to "couch-potato level."

Excite@Home teams with cable operators to market its services to 500,000 customers in the United States and Canada. The Excite portal, visited by more than 15 million users monthly, features search services, online shopping, and content on topics such as careers and travel. Excite Voicemail allows users to get free voice mail, e-mail, and fax messages from a single account.

Send resumes to:

Excite@Home
P.O. Box 92222
Los Angeles, CA 90009-2222
Phone their toll-free fax number
    (resumes only): 877-310-3326

You'll also be given an opportunity complete an online job application form at their Web site.

Exodus Communications

www.exodus.net
CEO Ellen M. Hancock
Employees 472
Tel: 408-346-2200
Fax: 408-346-2206
Santa Clara, CA
Cupertino, CA

Exodus is an Internet data center company providing facilities for total management of corporate Internet, Intranet and Extranet servers. Exodus provides businesses with all the tools they need to maintain the highest availability and performance for their mission-critical Internet operations 24 hours a day, 7 days a week.

Forward your resume, indicating position and location of interest, to:

Exodus Communications, Inc.
ATTN: Staffing Department
2831 Mission College Blvd.
Santa Clara, CA 95054

You can also fax: (310) 337-3340 or e-mail to: www.exodus@isearch.com. Exodus asks that you supply your resume in flat ASCII format and that you indicate position(s) and city/cities of interest on the subject line.

FileNET Corporation

www.filenet.com
CEO Lee D. Roberts
Employees 1,443
Tel: 714-966-3400
Fax: 714-966-3490
Costa Mesa, CA

A leading developer of computer-based imaging and workflow document management systems, FileNET Corporation develops, markets, and services an open, integrated family of workflow, document-imaging, electronic document-management, and computer output to laser disk ("COLD") client/server product solutions. These services and solutions control and manage the movement of document images, data, text, and other information throughout an enterprise.

Use the company Web site to check out the positions in which you're interested. You'll be able to e-mail your resume by clicking on the bottom of the job listing.

Fore Systems, Inc.

www.fore.com
CEO Thomas J. Gill
Employees 1,592
Tel: 412-772-6600
Fax: 412-742-7700
Warrendale, PA

FORE Systems, Inc., a subsidiary of U.K.-based manufacturing giant GEC, designs, develops, manufactures, and sells high-performance networking products based on ATM technology. FORE's networking products enable customers to connect computers to form clusters, workgroups, and LANs, to build backbones for enterprise-wide networks, and to provide transparent, end-to-end LAN and WAN connectivity.

You'll paste your resume into an e-mail sent directly to the person responsible for hiring.

Resumes can be sent to:

Marketing Recruiting
FORE Systems
1000 FORE Drive
Warrendale, PA 15086
Fax: (800) 394-0508

Gateway Computer

www.gateway.com
CEO Theodore W. Waitt
Employees 13,300
Phone: 605-232-2000
Fax: 605-232-2023
North Sioux City, SD

Formerly Gateway 2000, Gateway Computer, based in North Sioux City, South Dakota, is the number-two direct marketer of PCs in the United States, behind global leader Dell. Gateway provides products quickly and directly to computer users ordering by phone or Web site, instead of through resellers, cutting markup costs and speeding the release of new technology. The company makes desktop and portable PCs, PCTVs, and servers. Gateway also sells component add-ons such as CD-ROM drives and offers Internet access (gateway.net). Gateway continues to add to its more than 150 Country Store showrooms in the United States. About half of its products are sold to consumers.

Check out the recruitment page on their Web site. Applicants can submit their resumes via fax or regular mail, or use an online resume form available on the Web page. Gateway prefers that you e-mail your resume and cover letter in the body of the e-mail (or as attachments). Attachments should be in one of the following standard formats:

HTML
Microsoft Word (Mac or Windows), RTF, Works, Write, or Excel
WordPerfect (Mac or Windows)
Lotus Word Pro, AMI Pro or 1-2-3
ASCII or Unicode text (plain text)

Gemplus

www.gemplus.com
CEO Marc Lassus
Employees 2,919
Tel: 650-654-2900
Fax: 650-654-2914
Redwood City, CA

Gemplus is a provider of conventional and smart card-based solutions. Gemplus sells magnetic stripe cards, memory and microprocessor-based smart cards, smart contactless cards, electronic tags and smart objects. Gemplus designs and markets software, development tools, and readers. Gemplus also provides consulting, training, and personalization services to deliver the industry's most comprehensive and flexible card-based solutions to its developers, distributors, partners, and customers. With sales of over $648 million in 1998, Gemplus employs more than 4,300 people in ten manufacturing facilities, five R&D centers, and forty-one sales and marketing offices located in twenty-seven countries around the world.

Gemplus requests that you put your CV and cover letter in plain text in the body of the mail and not as an attachment. They stress that your CV will not be considered unless you follow these guidelines. For unsolicited applications, contact their Human Resources correspondents in Europe and Asia/Pacific regions.

GTE Corporation

www.gte.com
CEO Charles R. Lee
Employees 120,000
Phone: 972-507-5000
Fax: 972-507-5002
Irving, TX

GTE Corporation is a U.S.-based local telephone company. GTE's domestic and international operations serve 24.1 million access lines in the United States, Canada, the Dominican Republic, and Venezuela. Domestically, GTE is a mobile-cellular operator with the potential of serving 67 million cellular and personal communications service customers. Outside the United States, GTE operates mobile-cellular networks serving 15 million "POPs" through affiliates in Canada, the Dominican Republic, Venezuela, and Argentina.

The employment page gives instructions and addresses for you to contact their University Relations or Professional Recruitment staffing departments. They also suggest that you visit one of their employment centers for more information or to submit a cover letter and resume; you'll find the addresses listed by region.

Hewlett-Packard

www.hp.com
CEO Carly S. Fiorina
Employees 124,600
Tel: 415-857-1501
Fax: 415-857-5518
Palo Alto, CA

HP recently named a new CEO. It says mountains about the company that two women finished first and second in the race for the CEO's slot. Along with its consolidated subsidiaries, Hewlett-Packard Company, founded in 1939, designs, manufactures, and services equipment and systems for measurement, computation, and communications. The company is responsible for a wide variety of systems and stand-alone products, including computer systems, personal computers, printers and other peripheral products, calculators and other personal information products, electronic test equipment and systems, medical electronic equipment, solid-state components, and instrumentation for chemical analysis. Services such as systems integration, selective-outsourcing management, consulting, education, product financing and rentals, as well as customer support and maintenance, are also an integral part of Hewlett-Packards offerings.

Regardless of where you live or want to work, HP asks that you send your resume and cover letter to this e-mail address: resume@hp.com, or fax your resume to: (650) 852-8138. They also have an online employment application form that is available to expedite the resume submittal process. If you are applying for a specific job(s), indicate the event number and the job number(s) (listed with each job opening) clearly on your cover letter. HP sends all interviewees a letter confirming that their information is available online.

IBM

www.ibm.com
CEO Louis Gerstner Jr.
Employees 291,067
Tel: 914-449-1900
Fax: 914-765-7382
Armonk, NY

IBM develops, manufactures, and sells advanced information processing products, including computers and microelectronic technology, software, networking systems, and information technology-related services worldwide. IBM helps industry leaders and innovators in banking, manufacturing, retailing, communications, and many other fields use the Internet's power to get closer to their customers, increase revenues, extend their market reach, maximize their information resources, and work more productively. IBM offers services in helping companies at all stages of business needs in the area of electronic business. IBM has applications, services, and support to help a company with an existing or planned level of electronic activity and infrastructure. IBM can provide solutions that will build on a company's current systems, help create an in-house Internet-based business system, support business processes off-premises, or provide networked service offerings.

You can fill out a resume online at the company Web site, and it will be used to identify matches between current IBM job openings and any occurring in the next six months. They consider your job experiences, skills, and career interests. If a job match is identified, an IBM recruiting team member will contact you. If you have an existing resume that you would like to use, paste or type a "text only" (ASCII) version of your resume into their online form.

Informix Software, Inc.

www.informix.com
CEO Jean-Yves Dexmier
Employees 4,491
Tel: 415-926-6891
Fax: 415-926-6593
Menlo Park, CA

Founded in 1980 by Robert Sippl, Informix is one of the nation's largest database management software companies. Its core product is Informix Dynamic Server, which works in Unix and Windows operating environments. Other Informix products include applications development tools for creating client/ server production applications, decision support systems, ad-hoc query interfaces, and connectivity software that allows information to be shared transparently from PCs

to mainframes within the corporate computing environment.

You can submit your resume to:

Informix
Human Resources Dept.
1399 Moffett Park Dr.
Sunnyvale, CA 94089

Use an online resume form available on the company's employment Web page, located at www.informix.com. Send it to the attention of Human Resources via e-mail: jobs@infoseek.com

Infoseek

www.infoseek.com
CEO Harry M. Motro
Employees 319
Tel: 408-543-6000
Fax: 408-734-9350
Sunnyvale, CA

Infoseek develops and provides branded, comprehensive Web-based navigational services to Internet users, helping them access and personalize the immense resources of information on the World Wide Web. By forming a strategic alliance with The Walt Disney Company, Infoseek evolved from a simple search engine to the operator of the GO Network, a gateway to the Internet, which integrates Infoseek's search and directory services with several Disney-related Web sites. Aimed at individual users, Infoseek's primary service offering is Infoseek Guide, which is a free service. Infoseek Guide combines and packages the resources of the Internet to service the unique interests of the individual user. Infoseek also offers a directory of World Wide Web sites organized by topics.

Send Infoseek an e-mail to jobs@infoseek. com with your name, phone, e-mail and mailing address, and the job or job category in which you are interested. If you have an ASCII-formatted resume, please paste it in as well.

Infospace, Inc.

```
www.infospace-inc.com
CEO Naveen Jain
Employees 70+
Tel: 650-685-3000
Fax: 650-685-3001
San Mateo, CA
```

Infospace, Inc., is the market leader in scalable solutions for Web-based enterprise decision support and data publishing. Written completely in 100 percent Java, Infospace offers access and interactive visual analysis of data from any OLAP or relational database, data mart, or data warehouse from within a Web browser. Their products target the needs of Fortune 1000 companies with the most demanding database and World Wide Web requirements

Inktomi

```
www.inktomi.com
CEO David Peterschmidt
Employees 205
Tel: 650-653-2800
Fax: 650-653-2801
San Mateo, CA
```

Inktomi develops and markets scalable software designed for the world's largest Internet infrastructure and media companies. The company's innovative software delivers high performance and scalability at significant cost savings by leveraging Inktomi's parallel and cluster computing technologies. Inktomi's applications include carrier-class network cache systems and the world's largest search engines.

To apply for any positions listed at their Web site, e-mail your resume to

inktomi@inktomijobs.com

Intel

```
www.intel.com
CEO Craig R. Barrett
Employees 64,500
Tel: 408-765-8080
Fax: 408-765-9904
Santa Clara, CA
```

Its microprocessors, including the Pentium, have been providing the nerve center for IBM-compatible PCs since 1981. Intel continues to expand and upgrade its products and facilities to maintain its dominance over rival chipmakers. The company also makes computer flash memory chips, microcontrollers, and networking, communications, and graphics products. Intel has plants in China, Ireland, Israel, Malaysia, the Philippines, and the United States. About 55 percent of its sales are outside the United States.

Intermedia

```
www.intermedia.com
CEO David C. Ruberg
Employees 3,931
Phone: 813-829-0011
Fax: 813-349-9806
Toll Free: 800-250-2222
Tampa, FL
Cupertino, CA
```

Intermedia Communications provides integrated telecommunications solutions, including voice, data and multimedia, local and long-distance, and advanced access services, in cities throughout the United States. Its Digex subsidiary, which is to be spun off, provides business Internet connectivity and Web site management

Intermedia asks that you send your resume to salesresume@intermedia.com.

Mail your resume to:

Intermedia Communications
3625 Queen Palm Drive
Sabal VI Building
Tampa, FL 33619
Fax: (813) 829-7707

Interwoven

www.interwoven.com
CEO Martin Brauns
Employees 80
Tel: 650-917-3600
Fax: 650-917-3603
Los Altos, CA

Interwoven, Inc., develops and markets solutions for industrial-strength Web site production control. Interwoven's solutions are designed for large, complex Internet and intranet Web operations maintained by multiple development teams and potentially thousands of content contributors distributed throughout the enterprise.

Interwoven asks that you please fax your cover letter and resume to (408) 774-2002 or send them via e-mail to the addresses provided.

Intuit

www.intuit.com
CEO William Harris Jr.
Employees 2,860
Phone: 650-944-6000
Fax: 650-944-3699
Mountain View, CA

Intuit, Inc., founded in 1983, has become the largest manufacturer of accounting, personal finance, and tax software in the United States.

It develops and markets Quicken personal finance software, TurboTax tax preparation software, and QuickBooks small business accounting software. Intuit's Quicken Financial Network (http://www.qfn.com) offers news, information and market spaces (including the mutual fund Web site, NETworth.galt.com), and the personal insurance Web site, Quicken InsureMarket.com.

Check out the opportunities, select a job, and fill out their online application.

Lawson Software

www.lawson.com
CEO Richard Lawson
Employees 1,600
Tel: 612-379-2633
    or 800-477-1357
Fax: 612-379-7141
Minneapolis, MN

Lawson Software is a full-service provider of enterprise-wide, client/server business application solutions. Lawson's systems can assist companies in the management of financial and capital resources, personnel-related information, and the distribution of materials and inventory. Lawson incorporates technologies like client/server, GUI, and multiple RDBMSs to provide a true open solution. Lawson Software offers the following product lines: LAWSON INSIGHT Financial Management System, LAWSON INSIGHT Human Resources System, Open Enterprise Distribution Management System, and Open Enterprise Materials Management System.

Level 3 Communications

www.level3.com
CEO James Q. Crowe
Employees 8,000
Phone: 402-536-3677
Fax: 402-536-3632
Omaha, NB
Cupertino, CA

Level 3 offers local, long-distance, and Internet service over leased network capacity in fifteen cities in the United States and two in Europe. The company, a spin-off of construction giant Peter Kiewit Sons, also offers computer operations outsourcing and owns stakes in telecom providers RCN and Commonwealth Telephone Enterprises. It is building an international fiber-optic network based on Internet protocol (IP) technology, in which McCaw-controlled entities, including Nextel and Nextlink, are investing in return for network capacity.

E-mail your resume as an attachment to Jobs@Level3.com in either text or Word format. Resumes will only be accepted if they specifically reference a Req. ID in the subject line. If you are unable to submit your resume via e-mail, you can fax it to (888) 545-9407. Be sure to include the position's Req. ID number on the cover sheet of your fax. See the company's Web site for instructions on applying for a position in Europe.

Lucent Technologies

www.lucent.com
CEO Richard A. McGinn
Employees 136,000
Tel: 908-582-8500
Fax: 908-508-2576
Murray Hill, NJ

Lucent Technologies was created in 1996 as part of AT&T's decision to split into three separate companies. Lucent combines the systems and technology units that were formerly a part of AT&T with the research and development capabilities of Bell Labs. Lucent Technologies, Inc., designs, develops, and manufactures telecommunications systems, software, and products. Lucent is a global seller of public telecommunications systems, and is a supplier of systems or software to twenty-three of the world's twenty-five largest network operators.

Before you can apply for any jobs online, Lucent will have you create an online resume at their site. After submitting your resume, they will contact you via e-mail to let you know that they received your resume. You can either manually enter your information into the appropriate fields in their form, or you can cut and paste your resume into the space provided using their Reslex system. Your information will be placed automatically into the appropriate fields for your review.

MCI WorldCom

www.wcom.com
CEO Bernard J. Ebbers
Employees 55,000
Tel: 202-872-1600
Fax: 202-887-3140
Washington, DC

MCI provides a wide range of long-distance telecommunication services, including basic long-distance telephone service; voice and data services over software-defined virtual private networks; private line services; collect calling, operator assistance and calling card services, including prepaid calling cards; toll free or 800 services; 900 services;

switched and dedicated Internet access services; and Internet backbone services. In April of 1997, MCI announced a definitive agreement to merge with WorldCom, declaring the new name of MCI WorldCom (1999 MCI merged with WorldCom).

Just fill out the electronic form to add your resume to their database. MCI WorldCom will keep your resume on file for 90 days, during which time it will be considered for employment opportunities with the company.

Micron Technology

www.micron.com
CEO Steven R. Appleton
Employees 11,400
Phone: 208-368-4000
Fax: 208-368-4435
Boise, ID

Micron Technology is the nation's third-largest direct seller of PCs (after Dell and Gateway) and the world's number-two maker of semiconductor memory components (after Samsung). Dynamic random-access memories (DRAMs) and other chips account for nearly half of Micron's sales. Micron has shifted production from 16-megabit to 64-megabit DRAMs and has broadened its product lines to include embedded memory for the digital video market and a radio-frequency identification chip that helps track parcels.

Paste your ASCII text resume, or attach your Word or Wordperfect formatted resume into an e-mail and forward it to: pers-records@micron.com. If you are interested in a specific position, be sure to include the job title and/or job code found on the job posting. If you are not responding to a specific position, indicate your preferred division/group and location.

Microsoft

www.microsoft.com
CEO William Gates III
Employees 22,276
Tel: 425-882-8080
Fax: 425-936-7329
Redmond, WA

Microsoft develops, manufactures, licenses, sells, and supports a wide range of software products, including scalable operating systems for information appliances, personal computers, and servers; server applications for client/server environments; business and consumer productivity applications; software development tools; and Internet and Intranet software and technologies. The Microsoft Network offers proprietary online content, and Microsoft's Internet Explorer browser is used by online services and on corporate intranets.

When beginning the application process, Microsoft needs only your name, contact information, and recent job history, though you may provide additional information if you wish.

You'll be given a choice of the following options:

Build your resume with their online Resume Builder

E-mail your resume in ASCII text format to resume@microsoft.com

Mail your resume to:

Microsoft Corporation
Attn: Recruiting
One Microsoft Way, Ste. 303
Redmond, WA 98052-8303

Please note job title and code of the position(s) you are applying for. Note: Do not include attachments within the Resume Builder. If you have any attachments, e-mail them to resume@microsoft.com.

MindSpring Enterprises

www.mindspring.com
CEO Charles M. Brewer
Employees 1,600
Tel: 404-815-0770
Fax: 404-815-0082
Atlanta, GA

MindSpring is an Internet service provider focusing on delivering remarkable service and support to its customers. By following its core values and beliefs, MindSpring is committed to doing an exceptional job of serving its customers, its employees, its owners, and its community. MindSpring's dial-up subscribers can browse the World Wide Web, send e-mail, participate in online chats, and access over 21,000 newsgroups. MindSpring offers local Internet service in more than 320 locations throughout the United States and is also a provider of Web hosting services and domain registrations.

Moai Technologies, Inc.

www.moai.com
CEO Anne Perlman
Employees 35
Tel: 415-490-5550
Fax: 415-490-4823
San Francisco, CA

Moai Technologies, Inc., provides enterprise-level software applications for elec-

tronic commerce. Moai's flagship product, LiveExchange, enables corporations to host their own Web-based inventory auctions. Using Moai's technology, a company can create its own virtual private marketplace, where only select trading partners can participate in inventory auctions. The company has focused on providing solutions for selling excess and end-of-life inventory in the computer, component and semiconductor markets.

MOAI has a detailed listing of their openings with complete job descriptions for each position. Forward your resume to jobs@moai.com. Be sure to include their job reference number with your resume submission.

NCR

www.ncr.com
CEO Lars Nyberg
Employees 38,500
Phone: 937-445-5000
Fax: 937-445-1682
Dayton, OH

NCR delivers commercial open computer systems for transaction processing and decision-support solutions to customers in all industries. NCR's primary operating units are Retail Industry Solutions (POS systems), Financial Industry Solutions (payment systems, global leader in ATMs), National Accounts Solutions (data warehousing), and Systemedia Group (ribbons and other media products).

You'll fill out an online form when you select a job for which you'd like to apply. You'll be given space to paste in sections of your resume, too.

Netcom Systems

www.netcomsystems.com
CEO Barry Phelps
Employees 226
Phone: 818-700-5100
Fax: 818-709-0827
Chatsworth, CA

Netcom Systems developed the award-winning SmartBits systems, which have become the industry standard for network performance analysis for Ethernet, ATM, Packet over SONET, Frame Relay, Token Ring, and QoS enabled networks. SmartBits hardware and supporting software applications are used by leading network equipment manufacturers, network service providers, corporate enterprises, and test laboratories to measure the performance and services of networks and network equipment.

E-mail your resume to hr@netcomsystems.com.

Fax your resume to (818) 676-2700.

Netscape Computer Corporation

www.aol.com
CEO James L. Barksdale
Employees 2,385
Phone: 415-254-1900
Fax: 415-428-4072
Mountain View, CA

Now part of America Online, Netscape Communications Corporation is a provider of open software for linking people and information over Intranets and the Internet.

Netscape develops, markets, and supports a suite of enterprise server and client software, development tools and commercial applications to create a single shared communications platform for network-based solutions. Netscape software is based on industry standard protocols and therefore can be deployed across a variety of computer operating systems, platforms, and databases and can be interconnected with traditional client/server applications.

You'll apply online once you choose your desired position. For immediate consideration, you can call the following number twenty-four hours per day, seven days per week: (877) AOL-2DAY.

Network Associates

www.nai.com
CEO William L. Larson
Employees 1,600
Tel: 408-988-3832
Fax: 408-970-9727
Santa Clara, CA

Network Associates, the tenth-largest software company in the world, is a new company comprised from the merger of several industry leaders, including McAfee and Network General. Network Associates has privacy and encryption software from PGP and system enhancement tools from Helix. Recent acquisitions have moved the company into hardware sales and encryption technology. Network Associates pioneered electronic distribution (originally with antivirus shareware).

E-mail your resume to Human Resources:

Information@mc.afee.com

Newbridge Networks

www.newbridge.com
CEO Terence Matthews
Employees 6,336
Phone: 613-591-3600
Fax: 613-591-3680
Toll Free: 800-343-3600
Kanata, Ontario Canada
Cupertino, CA

Newbridge Networks Corporation designs, manufactures, markets and services a comprehensive desktop-to-desktop family of networking products and systems that enables customers in more than 100 countries to access the power of multimedia communications. Newbridge Network sells its products in more than seventy-five countries, and customers include major telecoms such as AT&T, Deutsche Telekom, and Cable & Wireless; smaller telephone service providers such as Pacific Bell; telecom equipment makers such as Alcatel Alsthom and Siemens; and private network users such as the British Post Office.

Send your resume via fax or by post to the appropriate region listed on the Web site, or submit your resume through either the Resume Builder or Resume Cut and Paste on this site.

Nortel Networks Corporation

www.nortelnetworks.com
CEO John A. Roth
Employees 73,000
Toll Free: 800-466-7835
Fax: 905-863-8048
Brampton, Ontario Canada
Cupertino, CA

Giant of the north, Nortel Networks (formerly Northern Telecom) is North America's number-two maker of telecommunications products behind Lucent. Northern Telecom (Nortel) manufactures telecommunications-related products such as telephone switching systems, telephone transmission systems, multimedia communications systems, PBXs, and mobile telecommunications equipment. Its international branches are Nortel North America and Nortel World Trade.

You'll need to access the company's Web site and apply online. Note that you need only to submit one resume to Nortel Networks, as all hiring managers are able to access your application. If you are applying for a New Grad position and wish to reference several specific jobs, simply include the reference numbers of the positions in your cover letter to ensure your application is able to be matched to your positions of interest.

FYI: For the benefit of 2000 new graduates and students, Nortel has a "recommended application format" which helps to highlight the information that managers look for when reviewing applicants' resumes. Check out their recommendations thoroughly before you submit your resume.

Novell

www.novell.com
CEO Eric Schmidt
Employees 5,818
Tel: 801-222-6000
Fax: 801-453-1267
Norem, UT

Founded in Utah in 1980, an estimated 55 million people now connect to more than three million Novell networks. More than half of all networks run on Novell software, most of which use the NetWare operating system. Novell software products include server operating systems, network applications, and distributed network services. These products enable businesses of all sizes to maintain distributed information resources across computer networks that integrate many different computers, operating systems, applications, and devices. Novell markets its products through forty U.S. and sixty-three international sales offices. Novell sells its products through distributors and national retail chains, which in turn sell the company's products to retail dealers.

Select a position from their list and then fill out an electronic resume. Your e-mail address is required if you expect a reply. If you do not have your resume in soft copy form, Novell asks that you please fax (in fine mode only) to (801) 861-7949.

Mail to:

Novell Inc.
Staffing Department
MS B131
122 East 1700 South
Provo, UT 84606
TDD: (801) 861-4881

Open Market, Inc.

www.openmarket.com
CEO Shikhar Ghosh
Employees 527
Phone: 781-359-3000
Fax: 781-359-8111
Burlington, MA

With offices in several countries, including Canada, Britain, France, Germany, Italy, the Netherlands, Japan, and Australia, Open Market's products are distributed by several of Japan's largest trading companies as well as by leading companies in other countries, such as Malaysia, Singapore, and South Africa. Open Market, Inc., develops, markets, licenses and supports high-performance software products that allow its customers to engage in business-to-consumer and business-to-business electronic commerce on the Internet and to construct Internet-based business applications within an enterprise. Transact, Open Market's flagship product, has been implemented by some of the world's most respected companies who are at the forefront of the information economy.

You can forward your resume to hiring @openmarket.com (URLs, ASCII, or HTML) or to:

Hiring Department
Open Market, Inc.
1 Wayside Road
Burlington, MA 01803

Oracle

www.oracle.com
CEO Lawrence J. Ellison
Employees 36,802
Phone: 650-506-7000
Fax: 650-506-7200
Redwood City, CA
Cupertino, CA

Founded in 1977 to take advantage of the technology first developed—and later fumbled—by IBM, Oracle immediately experienced rapid success and growth. In the early 1990s, it looked as if the company might not be able to handle its own rapid growth spurt, but it managed to rebound and is back on the fast track. Oracle Corporation is an independent supplier of software for information management. Oracle's primary information management products can be categorized into three predominate product groupings: Server Technologies, Application Development, and Business Intelligence and Business Applications.

E-mail your resume to: jobs@us.oracle.com.

PairGain Technologies

www.pairgain.com
CEO Michael Pascoe
Employees 640
Phone: 714-832-9922
Fax: 714-832-9924
Toll Free: 800-370-9670
Tustin, CA

PairGain Technologies is a provider of telecommunications products based on high-speed Digital Subscriber Line technology. PairGain designs, manufactures, markets, and supports products that allow telecommunications carriers and private network owners to more efficiently provide high-speed digital services to end users over the large existing infrastructure of unconditioned copper wires. PairGain is focusing on boosting its sales in areas where copper infrastructure is pervasive, particularly outside the United States.

Send your resume in care of Human Resources Manager

Fax: (714) 730-3199
E-mail: hr@pairgain.com

Paradyne

www.paradyne.com
CEO Andrew S. May
Employees 1,000
Tel: 813-530-2000
Fax: 813-530-8216
Largo, FL

Paradyne develops industry-defining technologies that facilitate high-speed network access for communications, computing products, TDM solutions, and sophisticated network management for commercial customers, IPSs, FRSPs, NSPs, and campus environments. Paradyne's broad competencies are in transmission technologies and applications, particularly digital signal processing, channel coding, and communication applications, combined with a thorough understanding of WAN design and local loop characteristics. With corporate headquarters in Largo, Florida, Paradyne has field sales offices located throughout the United States and regional offices in Canada, Hong Kong, Japan, Singapore, United Kingdom, and France. Paradyne's technical centers are located in New Jersey and Florida.

Phone.Com
(Formerly **Unwired Planet**)

www.phone.com
CEO Alain Rossmann
Employees 135
Tel: 650-562-0200
Fax: 650-817-1499
Redwood City, CA

A provider of open, scaleable software platforms, Phone.Com allows for secure, wireless Internet/Intranet access to Web-based information services and applications from mass-market handheld devices, such as mobile phones and PDAs. The company's network- and device-independent solution is designed to serve a worldwide community and has been embraced by wireless telecommunications leaders worldwide.

Phone.Com asks for principals only to apply—no agencies. Agency resumes won't be accepted and will be considered unsolicited resumes not subject to placement fees.

Forward resumes to:

jobs@corp.phone.com
Phone.com Recruiting
P.O. Box 288
Waltham, MA 02454-0288
Phone: (650) 562-0200
Fax: (650) 817-1690

FYI: All their positions require at least three years related experience, except where noted. Also, remember to reference the desired department code on your resume or cover letter.

Pitney Bowes

www.pitneybowes.com
CEO Michael J. Critelli
Employees 29,900
Phone: 203-356-5000
Fax: 203-351-6059
Stanford, CT

Pitney Bowes is the world's largest producer of postage meters (with 86 percent of the U.S. market). The company has a management services division that provides facilities and records management and document services, and a leasing service that finances other companies' purchases of office equipment. Pitney Bowes also makes other mailing equipment, as well as copiers and fax machines, and provides shipping and weighing systems.

Submit your resume by fax or hard copy mail in "text only" (ASCII) format to the specific contact assigned to each job description (e-mail addresses are available as well).

Pixar

www.pixar.com
CEO Steven P. Jobs
Employees 430
Tel: 510-236-4000
Fax: 510-236-0388
Richmond, California

Pixar, founded in 1986, is an Academy Award-winning computer animation studio creating a new generation of animated feature films. Pixar animation combines the creativity of some of the world's leading animators and story writers with an entirely new, three-dimensional animated look. Pixar's first movie, *Toy Story*, was released by The Walt Disney Company in November 1995 and is the world's first fully computer-animated feature film. *Toy Story* became the highest grossing film released in 1995.

Please send your resume along with a demo reel, credit list, and/or portfolio if applicable, to the following address.

Pixar Animation Studios
Attn: Recruiting
1001 West Cutting Blvd.
Richmond, CA 94804

Phone: (510) 236-4000
Job Hotline: (510) 412-6017
Fax: (510) 236-0388
E-mail: hr@pixar.com

QLogic

www.qlc.com
CEO H. K. Desai
Employees 255
Phone: 714-438-2200
Fax: 714-668-5008
Toll Free: 800-662-4471
Costa Mesa, CA
Denver, CO

The company makes integrated circuits and adapter boards that connect peripheral devices to computers. Its input/output subsystems handle data flow between computers and such peripheral devices as hard disk, tape, and CD-ROM drives. QLogic focuses primarily on products using the SCSI (small computer system interface) standard, but it is expanding its product line to include the higher-performance fibre channel standard. It also makes chips for the mass storage and server markets.

Most positions are based at the Costa Mesa, California, headquarters. If you meet the minimum qualifications for an opening and wish to be considered, the company encourages you to send them your resume via any of the following:

E-mail: hr@qlc.com
Fax: (714) 668-5055
Mail: QLogic Corporation
Attn: Human Resources
3545 Harbor Blvd.
Costa Mesa, CA 92626

QUALCOMM

www.qualcomm.com
CEO Irwin M. Jacobs
Employees 11,600
Phone: 619-587-1121
Fax: 619-658-2100
San Diego, CA

QUALCOMM keeps everyone's eyes and ears open. The company's code division multiple access (CDMA) technology, an industry standard for mobile communications, is used in cellular phones, wireless telephone system equipment, and satellite ground stations. Its OmniTRACS global positioning system is used by the trucking industry to monitor traveling truckers. In a joint venture with several companies, including Loral Space and Communications, QUALCOMM is developing the Globalstar system of low-orbiting satellites, which will offer telecommunications services around the world. QUALCOMM also publishes the popular Eudora e-mail software.

QUALCOMM is looking for individuals who thrive in a fast-paced environment and don't consider *change* a bad word. They have opportunities in the United States and worldwide. They even sponsor University Days during the school year, in which hundreds of students from campuses around the country are invited to spend a three-day weekend with QUALCOMM in San Diego or Boulder, CO. To listen to a recording of their job openings, call (619) 658-JOBS (5627).

You can also request an e-mail copy of the new postings. Apply via their Web site.

E-mail: resumes@qualcomm.com (simple
    ASCII text only, no Tex or NROFF, etc.)
Fax: (619) 658-2110
Mail: QUALCOMM Incorporated
Human Resources Dept.

P.O. Box 919013
San Diego, CA 92191-9013

Qwest Communications International, Inc.

www.quest.net
CEO Joseph P. Nacchio
Employees 8,700
Tel: 303-992-1400
Fax: 303-992-1724
Denver, CO

Qwest Communications International, Inc., the number-four U.S. long-distance provider, is a multimedia communications company building a high capacity, Internet Protocol (IP)-based fiber optic network for the new millenium. Utilizing the Qwest Macro CapacitySM Network, their mission is to enable customers to seamlessly exchange multimedia content—images, data, and voice—as easily as traditional telephone networks enabled voice communication.

You can fill out an online resume builder for the quickest way to submit your application.

Qwest's tracking system will accept resumes sent in text format. Send text-only e-mails to Recruiting@Qwest.net. Qwest also maintains an informative 24-hour Job Line: (888) 793-7811 or (888) Qwest11

RealNetworks

www.real.com
CEO Robert Glaser
Employees 326
Phone: 206-674-2700
Fax: 206-674-2699
Toll Free: 888-768-3248
Seattle, WA
Cupertino, CA

RealNetworks (formerly known as Progressive Networks) was the pioneer in streaming software that allows audio and video products of broadcasters to be delivered over the World Wide Web in real time. It is used by more than sixty million Web surfers who can download the software for free. Almost 75 percent of RealNetworks' sales are in North America.

E-mail your resume to:

obs@real.com

Remedy Corporation

www.remedy.com
CEO Lawrence Garlick
Employees 764
Tel: 650-903-5200
Fax: 650-903-9001
Mountain View, CA

Remedy develops and markets adaptable applications for the consolidated operations management market. Remedy Corporation is the number-one maker of help desk management software for corporate networks. Used as an internal help desk application, the company's Action Request System tracks and resolves support requests and problems in Windows and high-performance Unix computing environments.

Remedy Corporation/Employee Services
1505 Salado Drive
Mountain View, CA 94043
Fax: (650) 254-4900
E-mail: success@remedy.com

Renaissance Worldwide

www.rens.com
CEO G. Drew Conway
Employees 6,000
Phone: 617-527-6886
Fax: 617-965-4807
Toll Free: 888-377-9119
Newton, MA
Cupertino, CA

An information technology consulting firm, Renaissance Worldwide (formerly The Registry), operates about ninety offices in the United States, Europe, and Asia. Renaissance Worldwide is now a full-service provider, offering professional services, corporate and systems strategies, and software and hardware installation solutions. The company targets corporations, primarily in the telecommunications, financial, manufacturing, and pharmaceutical industries, as well as government agencies.

Send your resume as an attached file. Use your browser or desktop mail application to send e-mail with the file attached. You'll click on the e-mail address of the appropriate contact, then you'll be instructed to include various codes pertaining to the desired position. You can paste your resume into their online form.

SAP AG

www.sap.com
CEO Hasso Plattner
Employees 13,000+
Phone: +49-6227-7-47474
Fax: +49-6227-7-57575
Waldorf, Germany
Cupertino, CA

Founded in 1972, SAP is based in Waldorf, Germany, and employs more than 13,000 people at offices in more than fifty countries worldwide. SAP is the only non-American contender among the world's five largest software producers. A market and technology provider of client/server enterprise application software, SAP America provides comprehensive solutions for any size company throughout the industry sectors. A strategic alliance with Microsoft turned Internet and Intranet commerce into a profitable reality, with SAP's R/3 business processes available on a common platform online. Both consumer-to-business and business-to-business transactions can be conducted completely electronically. Send your resume to the attention of Human Resources

Fax: (888) 672-6726
E-mail: staffing.america@sap-ag.de

SAS Institute

www.sas.com
CEO James H. Goodnight
Employees 5,400
Tel: 919-677-8000
Fax: 919-677-4444
Cary, NC

SAS Institute provides an integrated suite of information delivery tools that allow companies to transform the wide variety of data within their organization into information that business users need to make decisions. It's the world's largest privately held software company and has about 3.5 million users in roughly 120 countries.

Indicate the position number and title of interest and forward a resume and/or application to Department MOS. To build a resume tailored for SAS Institute, see their list for things they'd like to know about you. Include those items on your application.

1. Where did you go to school?
2. The all-important question: What's your major?
3. Where have you worked?
4. What are some extra skills or qualifications you've picked up along the way?
5. Earned any awards? Let us know! Remember you're selling yourself!
6. How about computer skills?
7. Lastly, let us know how to get in touch with you.

If there is anything else you can think of or want to include, put it in!

SBC Communications

www.sbc.com
CEO E. E. Whitacre Jr
Employees 129,850
Tel: 408-996-1010
San Antonio, TX

SBC Communications is the nation's second-largest diversified telecommunications company and a wireless communication provider. Through its subsidiaries, SBC provides innovative telecommunications products and services under the Southwestern Bell, Pacific Bell, Nevada Bell, and Cellular One brands. SBC gives you the choice of building your online resume at their site, or you can send your resume via U.S. mail to:

SBC Communications Inc.
Staffing Center
Room 9-Q-1
111 Soledad, Suite 150
San Antonio, TX 78205-2212

A direct e-mail message can be sent to sbcempl@corp.sbc.com

The Charles Schwab Corporation

www.schwab.com
CEO Charles R. Schwab
Employees 13,300
Phone: 415-627-7000
Fax: 415-627-8840
San Francisco, CA

Schwab has been an extremely hot firm in recent years. In 1998, its revenues rose 20 percent, while its net income shot up 30 percent. Customers invest about $500 billion through Schwab. Although part of the reason the firm has grown is its alliances with investment banks J. P. Morgan, Credit Suisse First Boston (CSFB), and Hambrecht & Quist, the major reason for Schwab's rapid ascension is its dominance of online trading. According to *The New York Times,* the firms' computing center in Phoenix handles about a third of all Internet trading. The firm is moving quickly toward offering full brokerage services online and dispensing advice and research through its Web site. Schwab is also exploring more creative uses of the Internet, such as e-mailing clients with news based on their investment preferences.

E-mail your resume to:

schwab.jobs@schwab.com

Science Applications International (SAIC)

www.saic.com
CEO J. Robert Beyster
Employees 35,200
Phone: 619-546-6000
Fax: 619-546-6800
San Diego, CA

Science Applications International (SAIC), founded in 1969, has built its business practice upon increasingly complex scientific and engineering contracts with the Department of Defense. SAIC has played a role in high-profile projects from the cleanup of Three Mile Island to the construction of the Hubble Space Telescope. Government contracts currently account for two thirds of SAIC's business, more than half of which is directly related to matters of national security. With more than 150 locations, SAIC provides scientific and engineering services to major U.S. and foreign corporations. The company's current services include software development, computer system development and integration, tech support, and others.

Go to their Web site, which is updated regularly. It offers applicants the opportunity to submit their resumes electronically, the method of resume submission that SAIC prefers.

Siebel Systems, Inc.

www.Siebel.com
CEO Thomas Siebel
Employees 1,700
Tel: 650-295-5000
Fax: 650-295-5111
San Mateo, CA

Siebel Systems, Inc., is an industry provider of enterprise-class sales and marketing information software systems. Siebel designs, develops, markets, and supports Siebel Sales Enterprise, an Internet-enabled, object-oriented client/server application software product family designed to meet sales and marketing information system requirements. Glaxo Wellcome, Prudential Insurance, and Lucent Technologies are listed among Siebel's global clientele.

Send your resume and include a cover letter that states your salary requirements. You can e-mail your resume to careers@siebel.com, or you can fax it at (650) 295-5119.

Silicon Graphics, Inc.

www.sgi.com
CEO Richard E. Belluzzo
Employees 10,286
Phone: 650-960-1980
Fax: 650-932-0661
Mountain View, CA

A manufacturer of high-performance visual computing systems, Silicon Graphics delivers interactive three-dimensional graphics, digital media, and multiprocessing supercomputing technologies to technical, scientific, and creative professionals. Its subsidiary, MIPS Technologies, Inc., designs and licenses the industry's RISC processor technology for the computer systems and embedded control markets.

Silicon Graphics' jobs page contains a tool that will allow you to submit your resume against existing job positions. All resumes submitted against a specific position will also be entered into SGI's resume tracking system. You'll also be given the option to submit your resume independent of any of the existing positions through the resume tracking system.

Sprint

www.sprint.com
CEO William T. Esrey
Employees 64,900
Phone: 913-624-3000
Fax: 913-624-3088
Westwood, KS

With more than 7.6 million lines in eighteen states, Sprint is the number-two non-Baby Bell local-service phone company (after GTE) and trails only AT&T and MCI WorldCom in the race for U.S. long-distance markets. As *Internet Jobs!* went to press, MCI WorldCom, the nation's second largest long-distance phone company, announced it was acquiring Sprint in a deal valued at $115 billion, making it the largest corporate acquisition in U.S. history.

Sun Microsystems

www.sun.com
CEO Scott G. McNealy
Employees 26,300
Tel: 650-960-1300
Fax: 650-969-9131
Palo Alto, CA

Sun introduced the computer language Java in May 1995 as a way to animate features on Web pages. A supplier of enterprise network computing products, including desktop systems, servers, storage subsystems, network switches, software, and microprocessors, Sun Microsystems offers a full range of services and support. Sun's products are used for many demanding commercial and technical applications in various industries. The company conducts its business through various operating entities and divisions organized around the principal areas of added value. Each of the businesses generally operates separately within their charters, but with the common corporate strategic vision of being a leading force in network computing, which Sun believes allows it to more efficiently focus on its customers and the products, channels, and markets necessary to serve them.

Sybase

www.sybase.com
CEO John S. Chen
Employees 4,196
Tel: 510-922-3500
Fax: 510-922-3210
Emeryville, CA

Sybase, Inc., is a worldwide provider of distributed, open computing solutions. Sybase provides customers and partners with software and services to create business solutions for strategic competitive advantage. Sybase designs and develops products geared toward open, distributed, high-performance, end-to-end solutions which include databases, middleware, and application development tools for client/server, Internet and Intranet transaction processing, and data mart and data warehousing applications.

Symbian

www.symbian.com
CEO Colly Myers
Employees 250
Phone: 215-255-1200
Fax: 215-255-1002
London, England

Symbian owns, licenses, develops, and supports the EPOC platform, providing leading software, user interfaces, application frameworks, and development tools for Wireless Information Devices such as Communicators and Smartphones.

Enclose a cover letter stating why you are suitable for the position, your current salary, the reference for the job for which you are applying, and enclose your CV/Resume. For positions in the United Kingdom, you must be a resident of the U.K. or hold a valid work visa:

HR Department
Symbian Ltd
Sentinel House
16 Harcourt Street
London
W1H 1DS
U.K.
Fax: +44 171 2081866

E-mail to jobs@symbian.com. For U.K. vacancies, make sure that you include the previous information and attach your CV/Resume.

Telcordia

www.bellcore.com
CEO Richard Smith
Employees 5,270
Phone: 973-829-2000
Fax: 973-829-3172
Morristown, NJ
Cupertino, CA

Created as the research unit for the seven Baby Bells during AT&T's 1984 breakup, Telcordia was then known as Bell Communications Research (Bellcore). After becoming a subsidiary of defense contractor Science Applications International, and with research only about 10 percent of its work, the company changed its name and began focusing on Internet-based technology. Clients include AT&T, GTE, and PCS Group.

You'll be asked to submit your resume online, with the following instructions: Electronic resumes are automatically sent to their scanner system. It is important to use ASCII text with no attachments. Paper copies received via regular mail are scanned using an optical scanner. Faxes make poor originals. It is difficult to scan them into the system.

Mail resumes to:

Human Resources
Telecordia Technologies
445 South St.
Morristown, NJ 07960-6438

Tellabs

www.tellabs.com
CEO Michael J. Birck
Employees 4,980
Tel: 630-378-8800
Fax: 630-852-7346
Lisle, IL

Tellabs designs, manufactures, markets, and services voice and data transport and network access systems that are used worldwide by public telephone companies, long-distance carriers, alternate service providers, cellular and other wireless service providers, cable operators, government agencies, and businesses. Its TITAN digital cross-connect system (about 60 percent of sales) helps connect incoming and outgoing lines.

Tellabs products are sold in both the domestic and international marketplaces through the field sales force and selected distributors to a major customer base.

Whether you are looking for an internship/co-op position or a permanent position at Tellabs, you may send your resume and cover letter to:

College Relations Program
Tellabs College Relations Program
Dept. JCIN
1000 Remington Blvd. MS 147
Bolingbrook, IL 60440
Fax: (516) 342-5737
E-mail: collegegraduates@tellabs.com

Texas Instruments

www.ti.com
CEO Thomas J. Engibous
Employees 35,948
Tel: 972-995-2011
Fax: 972-995-4360
Dallas, TX

Texas Instruments is engaged in the development, manufacture, and sale of a variety of products in the commercial electronics and electrical industry primarily for industrial and consumer markets. These products consist of components, digital products, and metallurgical materials. TI's business is based principally on its broad semiconductor technology and application of this technology to digital solutions for the networked society. Texas Instruments Incorporated is a high-technology company with sales or manufacturing operations in more than thirty countries.

TI offers you the choice of building an online resume at their Web site or pasting your existing resume (ASCII text only) into their form, which will automatically be e-mailed to them (they caution you, however, that resumes pasted directly out of word processors may cause inadvertent characters). You can also e-mail them directly to: resume1@ti.com (send ASCII text only, do not send formatted text such as a word processor document).

On September 10, 1996, Time Warner deployed the first commercial broadband online service to customers through a hybrid fiber/coaxial cable network linked to the end user's personal computer by a high-speed cable modem. Time Warner brings to this venture a unique collaborative product, developed by drawing upon the technological expertise of Time Warner Cable, the vast journalistic resources of Time, Inc., and the talent of Warner Brothers. Developed by a joint venture between Time Warner Cable and Time, Inc., Road Runner was conceived to be much more than a high-speed Internet access provider. Now the Pegasus program will provide Time Warner Cable customers with the next generation of advanced digital programming.

Prepare a resume and cover letter explaining what type of job you would like to obtain. Submit your application directly to the Human Resources department of the company or companies that most interest you. (Note: Turner Broadcasting System, Inc., includes TBS Superstation, CNN, TNT, and Cartoon Network.) You may call, fax, or mail in your application (no e-mail unless otherwise indicated). In most cases you can expect to receive a letter informing you that your application has been received or a call if your application matches an available position.

Time Warner

www.timewarner.com
CEO Gerald M. Levin
Employees 67,500
Tel: 212-598-7200
Fax: 212-420-4809
New York, NY

Trend Micro, Inc.

www.trendmicro.com
CEO Steve Chang
Employees 500+
Tel: 408-257-1500
Fax: 408-257-2003
Cupertino, CA

Trend Micro is a developer of server-based virus protection, with products designed for file servers, Internet and Intranet gateways, and e-mail servers. Trend Micro's virus protection software supports NetWare and Windows NT as well as Sun Solaris, HP-UX, and four other Unix operating systems. Trend Micro's products are sold directly as well as through authorized resellers worldwide and through OEM relationships.

At their Web site you can tell them a little about yourself via their online form, e-mail a plain text (ASCII) version of your resume, or fax or mail your resume (be sure to include the location and job code) to:

Fax: (408) 257-2003, Attention Hiring
    Manager
Mail: Trend Micro, Inc.
Attn: Hiring Manager
10101 N. De Anza Blvd., Suite 400
Cupertino, CA 95014

Trilogy Software

www.trilogy.com
CEO Joe Liemandt
Employees 400
Phone: 512-794-5900
Fax: 512-794-8900
Austin, TX

Trilogy Software makes products that computerize the process of ordering goods. Used by businesses and online shoppers, its software enables them to buy everything from computers to airplanes. Its products include Selling Chain (point-of-sale software for field and Internet sales), Buying Chain (procurement software), Marketing Chain (for tracking marketing plans), and Opportunity Manager (contract tracking software). Cus-

tomers include IBM, Ericsson, and GE. Trilogy's majority-owned spinoff, pcOrder.com, makes software that is used to sell computers over the Internet.

Trilogy recently outsourced a significant amount of its recruiting to recruiting startup CollegeHire.com. If you attend one of the schools listed, contact CollegeHire.com (*www.collegehire.com*) to pursue employment with Trilogy:

UC Berkeley
Brown
Cal Tech
CMU
Columbia
Cooper Union
Cornell
Dartmouth
Duke
Georgia Tech
Harvard
Harvey Mudd
Johns Hopkins
MIT
Princeton
Purdue
RPI
Rice
Stanford
UCLA
UIUC
University of Michigan
University of Pennsylvania
University of Southern California
University of Texas
University of Virginia
University of Wisconsin
Virginia Tech
Waterloo
Yale

You can submit your resume by mail, fax, or as an e-mail attachment (preferably in Microsoft Word, HTML, or plain text format):

Trilogy Recruiting
6034 West Courtyard Drive
Austin, TX 78730
Tel: (512) 794-5900
Fax: (512) 794-8900
recruiting@trilogy.com

U S WEST

www.uswest.com
CEO Solomon D. Trujillo
Employees 54,483
Phone: 303-793-6500
Englewood, CO

U S WEST, formerly U S WEST Communications Group, provides local phone service to more than 25 million customers in fourteen western and midwestern U.S. states. By upgrading its telephone network, striving to strengthen customer service, and entering new businesses, such as wireless personal communications services (PCS), it is preparing thoughtfully for increased competition.

Vantive Corp.

www.vantive.com
CEO Thomas L. Thomas
Employees 592
Tel: 408-982-5700
    or 800-582-6848
Fax: 408-982-5710
Santa Clara, CA

The Vantive Corporation is a provider of integrated customer interaction software. Companies such as Hewlett-Packard and Sears use Vantive's software to track complaints filed by customers, follow up on product information requests, and check the status of orders, among other tasks. These applications, called Vantive Enterprise, are based on a client/server architecture and common data model and can be used independently or as part of an integrated enterprise-wide customer information system.

After selecting the position you're applying for, you'll e-mail your resume to:

jobs@jobs.vantive.com

Visual Networks

www.visualnetworks.com
CEO Scott E. Stouffer
Employees 100+
Tel: 301-296-2300
Fax: 301-296-2301
Rockville, MD

Visual Networks, Inc., provides premium WAN service-level management systems, a new breed of WAN system that integrates expert WAN monitoring functionality with WAN access equipment. These systems automate site-to-site support and management of networks based on public data services such as frame relay, the Internet, and ATM.

You can mail or fax a resume to:

Human Resources
Visual Networks, Inc.
2092 Gaither Road
Rockville, MD 20850
Fax: (301) 296-2314
E-mail: jobs@visualnetworks.com

Be sure to indicate the position title you're interested in on the outside of your envelope, on your fax cover sheet, or in your e-mail.

Vitria Technology, Inc.

www.vitria.com
CEO JoMei Chang
Employees 157
Tel: 415-237-6900
Fax: 415-237-6920
Mountain View, CA

Vitria Technology, Inc., develops and markets software that enables breakthrough improvements in the speed and accuracy of business execution based on realtime, networked information. The maker of enterprise application integration software, Vitria lets software applications in large corporations communicate with each other, integrate stovepipe applications, analyze realtime data streams, and automate critical business processes. In addition to products and technology, Vitria offers a full range of consulting and professional services.

To apply, send your resume to Human Resources:

E-mail: bcsmith@vitria.com
Fax: (650) 237-6977

Whistle Communications

www.whistle.com
CEO John Hamm
Employees 75+
Tel: 650-577-7000
Fax: 650-577-7005
Foster City, CA

With an appliance the size an ordinary clock radio called the InterJet, Whistle Communications hopes to improve the ability of small offices to connect to the Net. The Interjet is described by the company as an "innovative all-in-one, affordable, network office device that delivers Internet productivity to everyone in a small office of up to 100 employees."

Whistle suggests that you e-mail your resume in plain text (ASCII) to:

jobs@whistle.com
Fax to: (650) 577-7041
Send to:
Whistle Communications
Attn: Human Resources
110 Marsh Drive
Foster City, CA 94404

Xylan Corporation

www.xylan.com
CEO Steve Y. Kim
Employees 1,044
Phone: 818-880-3500
Fax: 818-880-3505
Toll Free: 800-995-2612
Calabasas, CA
Cupertino, CA

Xylan Corporation, a subsidiary of French telecom group Alcatel, is a provider of high-bandwidth switching systems that enhance the performance of existing local area networks and facilitate migration to next-generation networking technologies such as ATM. Xylan Corporation is a provider of complete campus switching systems, including LAN switching, ATM switching, and Internetworking. Xylan's OmniSwitch connects Ethernet, Token Ring, FDDI, Fast Ethernet, ATM, and frame relay, using automatic any-to-any translation.

Fax (818) 880-3505 or e-mail (jobs@xylan. com) your resume (in ASCII plain text).
Mail to:

Xylan Corporation
26801 W. Agoura Road
Calabasas, CA 91301
Attn: Human Resources

Yahoo!

www.yahoo.com
CEO Timothy Koogle
Employees 803
Tel: 408-731-3300
Fax: 408-731-3301
Santa Clara, CA

Yahoo! is a customized online database designed to serve the needs of users in the

Internet community. Yahoo! users are able to efficiently locate, identify, and edit material stored on the Internet. One of the few Internet players operating in the black, the service is judiciously organized into key categories. Through partnerships with local and national content providers, Yahoo! is able to offer users a true insider's view of a particular community and region. Access current job openings through Yahoo's employment Web page, located at www.yahoo.com/docs/hr. Applicants can submit a resume either by e-mail or by fax, but Yahoo! will not answer phone inquiries or accept mailed resumes.

PART 4
Appendixes

THE FIFTY HOTTEST NET PLACES TO LIVE AND WORK

It's tempting to think that our work in the Net Economy is not anchored in any specific time or place, but the reality is that we are physical beings with physical needs under physical conditions, and the laws of physics require us to live somewhere. Even those of us who have cashed in our stock options to buy a home at the beach, one in the mountains, and a villa in Tuscany can live in only one house at a time. Because we all have to live somewhere, it makes sense to choose wisely. Many of these places are outside the United States, which is consistent with the fact that the Net is a global phenomenon. This appendix lists the fifty hottest cities and areas for Net jobs and invites readers to the *Internet Jobs!* Web site for updated information and hot links. Hot links to all these cities are available at *www.jkador.com/netjobs*.

WHO MAKES WHAT IN THE NET ECONOMY?

Compensation information changes every hour in the Net Economy, and it is waste of good paper to offer salary information in a book. To gauge approximate salaries and developing compensation trends, this appendix offers comprehensive information based on surveys conducted by *InfoWorld Magazine*, the leading trade newspaper of the Net Economy.

LET'S CONTINUE THE CONVERSATION ON THE WEB

A book like this can only gloss the surface of resources available to understand careers in the Net Economy. If you really want to drill down, go to the central collaborative platform of the Net Economy; the *Internet Jobs!* Web site offers abundant opportunities to further extend the value of your investment in this book.

APPENDIX A

The Fifty Hottest Net Places to Live and Work

The centers of gravity of the Net Economy are constantly shifting. The following fifty cities and regions offer candidates a critical mass of opportunities for work and recreation. On *Internet Jobs!*'s Web site *www.jkador.com/netjobs* you will find up-to-date information on all these locations, including:

- Description
- Net culture
- Business outlook
- Leading employers
- Historical sites

- Colleges and universities
- Recreational opportunities
- Sports
- Climate
- Further links

Any list of the fifty hottest net places to live and work shifts as quickly as the Net Economy itself. The list currently includes the following cities and regions, but check the Web site for new cities and updated information on each.

1. Albuquerque, NM
2. Atlanta, GA
3. Austin, TX
4. Baltimore, MD
5. Berkeley, CA
6. Boise, ID
7. Boston, MA
8. Boulder, CO
9. Cambridge, MA
10. Charlotte, NC
11. Chicago, IL
12. Cincinnati, OH

13. Cleveland, OH
14. Dallas/Fort Worth, TX
15. Denver, CO
16. Des Moines, IA
17. Detroit, MI
18. Fairfax County, VA
19. Houston, TX
20. Indianapolis, IN
21. Las Vegas, NV
22. Kansas City, MO
23. Minneapolis/St Paul, MN
24. Middlesex County, NJ
25. Newark, NJ
26. New Haven/Bridgeport/ Stamford, CT
27. New York City, NY
28. Orange County, CA
29. Philadelphia, PA
30. Phoenix, AZ
31. Portland, OR

32. Raleigh/Durham/Chapel Hill, NC
33. Rochester, MN
34. San Diego, CA
35. San Francisco/Oakland, CA
36. St. Louis, MO
37. San Jose, CA
38. Seattle, WA
39. Washington, DC
40. Paris, France
41. Adelaide, South Australia
42. Melbourne, Victoria, Australia
43. Sydney, New South Wales, Australia
44. Bangalore, India
45. Berlin, Germany
46. Budapest, Hungary
47. Hong Kong
48. Singapore
49. London, England
50. Tel Aviv, Israel

APPENDIX B

Who Makes What in the Net Economy?

It pays to become business savvy, but new skills are just one factor to consider when evaluating IT compensation packages.

As corporate dependence on IT grows, IT professionals find themselves increasingly drawn into business decisions rather than simply implementing and maintaining technologies. Now it appears that companies are backing up their desire for business-savvy IT professionals with cash.

The 1999 *InfoWorld* Compensation Survey found that the average salaries for IT professionals who focus on both business and technology are higher than the average salaries for those at the same level who focus primarily on technology.

However, with crucial company projects depending on the expertise and hard work of the IT staff, managers trying to make sure their employees stay on board need to look beyond salaries. And the right types of compensation can be used to encourage employees to develop and apply new skills, including business skills. In our second annual survey of the salaries and benefits our readers receive, we asked about both new trends and traditional factors that affect IT professionals' compensation. The results of our survey can help companies and individuals look beyond simple averages to define a fair compensation package. In addition, we asked a random sample of our readers what they thought about their compensation and work environments; their comments appear throughout this report.

BUSINESS SKILLS PAY OFF

The salary difference between purely technical employees and those who also focus on business suggests that companies may be starting to connect their compensation with the business results that these hybrid employees achieve.

Do IT professionals focus on business or technology?

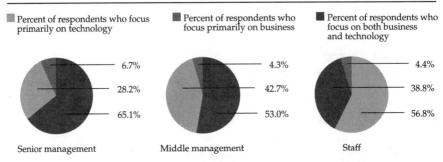

▪ Percent of respondents who focus primarily on technology	▪ Percent of respondents who focus primarily on business	▪ Percent of respondents who focus on both business and technology

Senior management — 6.7% — 28.2% — 65.1%

Middle management — 4.3% — 42.7% — 53.0%

Staff — 4.4% — 38.8% — 56.8%

"It used to be technical skills that got the job done," said an IT program designer at a government agency in California. "[Now] you must have the technical skills to accomplish the mission, but you must be proficient in business skills to obtain what is needed to accomplish the mission."

About half of survey respondents said they focus on a mixture of business and technology. Almost all of the rest said they focus primarily on technology; a small percentage said they focus primarily on business. Of those whose focus is split, an average of about 58 percent of their time is spent on technology and 42 percent on business.

The salary difference is greater the higher in management you go. For senior managers who focus on both business and technology, average salaries were 8.8 percent more than the average for those who focus primarily on technology; for middle managers, the difference was 6.8 percent. Even at the staff level there was a difference, although it was minor. Staff members who focus on both business and technology earned an average of 1.3 percent more than those who focus primarily on technology.

The overall message is that a joint focus on business and technology appears to be the best way to go for those who want the increased responsibility, salaries, and perks of senior management. And even at lower levels of the organization, it can pay off to develop business skills to complement technology skills.

For some groups, salary increases in the past year were also greater for those with a joint focus. In 1998 middle managers who focus on both business and technology reported average salary increases of 9.8 percent from the previous year; those who focus mainly on technology reported increases of 8.7 percent. For staff members, salary increases averaged 9.1 percent for those who focus on business and technology, compared with 8.2 percent for those who focus mainly on technology. IT business analysts reported one of the largest average salary increases—11.3 percent. And for senior managers, the salary increases each group reported were about the same—10.5 percent.

Many readers said the business portion of their jobs has been growing in recent years. Some also said they are happy about this. "If I invest my time and

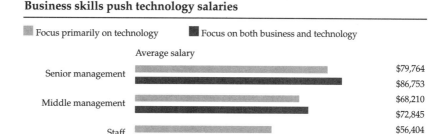

Business skills push technology salaries

◾ Focus primarily on technology ◾ Focus on both business and technology

Average salary

Senior management	$79,764
	$86,753
Middle management	$68,210
	$72,845
Staff	$56,404
	$57,139

energies in the creation of architecture, structure, or process, then I deserve to be heard when decisions are made concerning the use of those things," said an IT specialist at a state government department in Olympia, Washington.

However, some readers expressed concern about the difficulty of both keeping up with technology and developing business skills. "Too much focus on business would likely lead to me falling behind in technology," said a software engineer at a California-based software company.

Others equated focusing on business with delving into office politics, meetings, and busywork. "Bureaucratic papers, meetings, and such eat up so much time and resolve nothing that 30 percent of my production time is lost per week," said an IT program designer.

One respondent said that an increased business focus tends to accompany increased management responsibility, a trend that was borne out in our survey. "I'm happier with business because technology is just a supporting function," said an IT project manager at a mutual fund company in the Northeast.

TRADITIONAL MEASURES

Current trends such as the increased focus on business are not the only influence on salaries, of course. The charts on "Average salaries for IT professionals" which follow in this appendix, illustrate many of the factors that affect salary, including a company's size and location; the size of the budget or staff for which an IT professional is responsible; the industry; and education.

The education section of this appendix looks more closely at those degrees, especially MBAs, and delves into the contentious question of whether certification leads to more compensation. Whether they are tied to certification or not, salary increases are a hot issue for most people, and IT professionals did well in 1998: 85.4 percent of them reported salary increases, with an average increase of 9.3 percent.

A more interesting question might be whether changing companies is the way to a higher salary. Our data suggests that it is, but perhaps not to the extent that some people think. Given the hefty salary increases some IT professionals

A combined focus

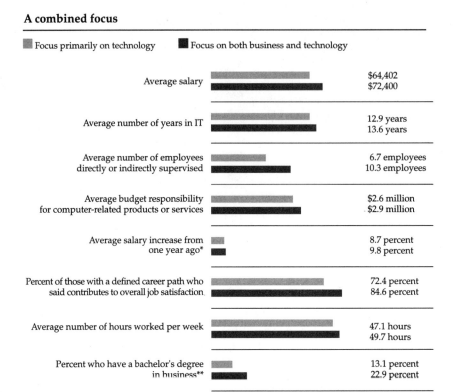

	Focus primarily on technology	Focus on both business and technology

Average salary	$64,402 / $72,400
Average number of years in IT	12.9 years / 13.6 years
Average number of employees directly or indirectly supervised	6.7 employees / 10.3 employees
Average budget responsibility for computer-related products or services	$2.6 million / $2.9 million
Average salary increase from one year ago*	8.7 percent / 9.8 percent
Percent of those with a defined career path who said contributes to overall job satisfaction	72.4 percent / 84.6 percent
Average number of hours worked per week	47.1 hours / 49.7 hours
Percent who have a bachelor's degree in business**	13.1 percent / 22.9 percent
Percent who have a bachelor's degree in computer science**	26.3 percent / 22.5 percent
Percent who have a master's degree in business**	7.8 percent / 13.4 percent

*Of those whose salaries increased
**Of those with a bachelor's degree or higher

report when they change jobs, it surprised us to find that people who have recently switched companies were not making much more than the overall average. A possible explanation is that companies might be starting to keep their salaries up to market rates.

FAIRNESS AND MOTIVATION

Perceptions about compensation can be almost as important as the compensation itself. We examine how well money works to motivate employees, as well as other key questions about the equity of IT salaries. For example, many people wonder if older workers and women get a fair shake in the IT job market. We looked at this issue in our survey and discovered that among survey respondents, on average, women senior managers are paid 78.6 percent of what their male counterparts make; women middle managers earn 82 percent of what men earn; and at the staff level, women earn 78.8 percent of what men earn. We also began to unravel the complicated relationships between age, experience, and salary, but these issues are more complicated than simply comparing numbers.

Another issue that is more complex than the numbers indicate is whether IT professionals are adequately compensated for the hours they put in. Some IT professionals work a forty-hour workweek, but many others are putting in long hours on the job and on call—some more happily than others. "The current pace is not sustainable over the long haul," said the director of worldwide IT support at a logistics company in California, who said that working sixty hours per week is considered part of the job.

"I have to keep everything working and do not have the tools available to keep things tuned automatically or remotely," said a system administrator at a west coast company, who works between fifty and sixty hours per week. "I receive no recognition, except from my wife for not being home enough."

Few respondents reported being paid extra to compensate directly for the extra work, and most reported getting extra time off infrequently at best. But some said they got rewards if they helped the business during those extra hours. "I'm not compensated solely for extra hours, but for business results achieved," said a technical sales specialist at a software company on the east coast who works between forty-five and fifty hours per week.

Flexibility seemed to make workers feel better about the long hours: 74.8 percent of the respondents who were offered flexible work hours said using this benefit contributed to their job satisfaction. "If I were to come in late after working late the night before, my manager would not say anything to me," said a programmer analyst at a manufacturing company in Pennsylvania. "She trusts my ethics."

USING THESE RESULTS

This survey is a guide to help you determine your staff's value—and your own. The survey used a strict random sample of our print subscribers and was completely confidential. In some cases, we did not get enough respondents in a particular category—database managers in the northeast, for example—to have stable projections. We have printed those answers and marked them with asterisks. They are not as reliable as the survey's other numbers, but consider them an alternative to asking a dozen or so of your colleagues around the country how much money they make and taking the average.

Keep in mind that surveys in general are imperfect tools for telling you exactly what you should be making. When you look at the salary charts, for example, remember that the national salary listed for CIOs is an average of numbers that range from about $30,000 to more than $300,000.

If you are an experienced middle manager at a large New York company that depends heavily on technology, and you have an MBA, a large budget, and many people reporting to you, you may well be due significantly more than the average listed for your job title in the northeast. However, if you live in a rural area of the same region, have a middle management title but are not responsible for many people or much money, do not have a college degree, and work for a small company that does not use technology heavily, a fair salary for you may be less than the average we report.

One of the best ways to use averages such as these is to compare them with the results of other surveys and look for patterns. The numbers reported in this survey, then, are an excellent starting point for your research into IT salaries; they are not by themselves the final answer.

AVERAGE SALARIES FOR IT PROFESSIONALS

How to Use These Numbers

It is tempting, when faced with charts of average salaries such as these, to try to find the one number that will tell you whether you are making enough money, or how much you should be paying your staff members. No compensation survey, however, can accurately take into account all variables that go into determining a fair salary.

A better use of salary charts is to examine the ways in which many different factors affect salaries. Look for patterns and use them to evaluate whether you should be making more or less than the average for your job in your region.

Average salaries for IT professionals

National and by region

Job title	National average	West[1]	Midwest[2]	South[3]	Northeast[4]
Senior management	**$87,514**	**$89,183**	**$89,244**	**$67,192**	**$99,451**
CIO/vice president of IT	$111,104	$119,005*	$112,589*	$69,272*	$131,886
Director of IT	$75,083	$82,540	$71,734	$66,865	$81,152
Other vice president/director	$96,262	$93,897*	$119,957*	$63,987*	$97,711*
Middle management	**$70,597**	**$68,935**	**$63,424**	**$65,042**	**$86,765**
Application development manager	$69,894	$71,421*	$65,691*	$73,070	$68,341
Database manager	$82,032	$66,210*	$67,055*	$83,432*	$101,801*
Help desk manager	$57,596	$59,611*	$40,333*	$61,694*	$56,550*
Internet/Web manager	$57,495*	$55,287*	$65,031*	$52,563*	$45,267*
IT manager	$68,619	$65,453	$65,560	$63,188	$78,918
IT project manager	$82,845	$76,656	$65,888*	$63,456	$130,333
Network manager	$61,656	$69,877*	$59,034	$53,488*	$66,445*

Average salaries for IT professionals (continued)

Staff	$57,054	$58,583	$52,111	$56,511	$61,973
Database analyst/administrator	$56,859	$56,785*	$54,828*	$58,804*	$57,171*
Help desk specialist	$49,986	$56,559*	$35,853*	$49,665*	$58,392*
Internet/Web developer	$61,409	$64,942*	$58,806*	$64,887*	$56,659*
IT business analyst	$63,183	$62,847*	$54,922*	$58,127*	$80,434*
Network/system administrator	$51,969	$49,219	$49,327	$48,938	$58,977
System programmer/analyst	$62,198	$67,025	$56,222	$61,309	$66,021

Metropolitan areas

	Chicago	Los Angeles/ San Diego	New York	Philadelphia/ Trenton	San Francisco/ San Jose
Senior management	$103,130*	$78,329*	$115,255	$94,772	$132,531*
Middle management	$66,408	$76,624*	$97,255	$74,420	$80,814*
Staff	$57,246*	$51,842*	$69,526	$63,390	$78,427*

Budget responsibility

	less than $100,000	$100,000– $399,999	$400,000– $999,999	$1 million– $4.9 million	$5 million– $9.9 million	$10 million or more
Senior management	$57,984	$68,198	$77,193	$93,901	$99,000	$157,000
Middle management	$55,473	$61,940	$66,918	$76,835	$99,571	$75,076
Staff	$51,048	$55,644	$57,374	$61,145	$74,200	$67,333*

Industry

	Business services	Computer-related manufacturing	Education	Finance/ insurance/ real estate/ legal services
Senior managment	$68,608	$118,829	$79,331	$88,877
Middle management	$63,957	$74,045	$71,985	$85,550
Staff	$60,379	$74,007	$38,504	$58,129

[1]West: Alaska, Arizona, California, Colorado, Hawaii, Idaho, Montana, Nevada, New Mexico, Oregon, Utah, Washington, and Wyoming

[2]Midwest: Illinois, Indiana, Iowa, Kansas, Michigan, Minnesota, Missouri, Nebraska, North Dakota, Ohio, South Dakota, and Wisconsin

[3]South: Alabama, Arkansas, Delaware, District of Columbia, Florida, Georgia, Kentucky, Louisiana, Maryland, Mississippi, North Carolina, Oklahoma, South Carolina, Tennessee, Texas, Virginia, and West Virginia

[4]Northeast: Connecticut, Maine, Massachusetts, New Hampshire, New Jersey, New York, Pennsylvania, Rhode Island, and Vermont

[5]Microsoft Certified Systems Engineer

[6]Certified Novell Engineer

[7]Promoted within company

* Numbers marked with an asterisk are based on fewer than 30 respondents and are unstable. Although they can be helpful indicators of the salaries for certain jobs, they may not be accurate projections of the average salaries for these categories.

InfoWorld, June 21, 1999. Used by permission.

BENEFITS

Bonuses

For many, financial rewards of IT work go beyond salaries. What's the best way to help employees see the link between IT work and business results? One possibility is to use bonuses to reward performance that helps the business.

IT professionals with a joint business-technology focus reported getting some kind of bonus in larger numbers than those who focus primarily on technology. For example, profit-sharing bonuses were the most common kind reported overall. Of the technically focused respondents who reported receiving bonuses, 49.8 percent said they received a profit-sharing bonus. Of those who focus on business and technology, 57.6 percent who reported bonuses got a profit-sharing bonus.

Other bonuses that suggest an alignment with achieving business results, including team performance bonuses and bonuses for the completion of a major project, showed a similar disparity. Of those who focus on business and technology and who reported bonuses, 12.5 percent said they received a team performance bonus, and 14.3 percent reported getting a bonus for the completion of a major project. Of those who focus primarily on technology and reported bonuses, 8.9 percent reported a team performance bonus, and 9 percent reported a bonus for the completion of a major project.

What employers offer, what employees like

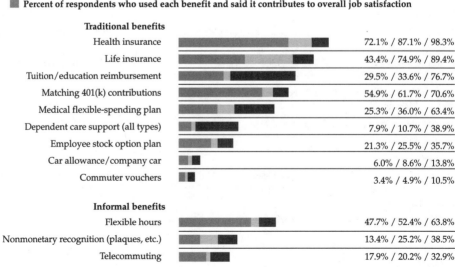

■ Percent of respondents who were offered each benefit
■ Percent of respondents who were offered and used each benefit
■ Percent of respondents who used each benefit and said it contributes to overall job satisfaction

Traditional benefits

Health insurance	72.1% / 87.1% / 98.3%
Life insurance	43.4% / 74.9% / 89.4%
Tuition/education reimbursement	29.5% / 33.6% / 76.7%
Matching 401(k) contributions	54.9% / 61.7% / 70.6%
Medical flexible-spending plan	25.3% / 36.0% / 63.4%
Dependent care support (all types)	7.9% / 10.7% / 38.9%
Employee stock option plan	21.3% / 25.5% / 35.7%
Car allowance/company car	6.0% / 8.6% / 13.8%
Commuter vouchers	3.4% / 4.9% / 10.5%

Informal benefits

Flexible hours	47.7% / 52.4% / 63.8%
Nonmonetary recognition (plaques, etc.)	13.4% / 25.2% / 38.5%
Telecommuting	17.9% / 20.2% / 32.9%

One exception to this pattern was the signing bonus. Of those who focus on technology and got a bonus in 1998, 7.3 percent reported receiving a signing bonus; of those whose focus is split and got a bonus last year, 6.2 percent reported a signing bonus. This relatively small difference may point to the high demand for specific technical skills in some areas.

Signing bonuses also appear to be the most lucrative bonuses to receive, although as with all averages, the average bonus numbers mask the fact that a few people reported extremely high signing bonuses, while many others got smaller amounts. The majority of the signing bonuses reported were between $5,000 and $10,000.

We asked respondents about a couple of other kinds of bonuses: those for new employee referrals and those for completing technical education or certification. Neither produced enough responses for us to have an accurate idea of how large the bonuses are, but the responses did indicate that IT professionals aren't getting these bonuses in large numbers.

It's important to remember that bonuses can also cause dissension, especially when the recipients (or those who did not receive a bonus) do not understand how bonuses are distributed. "No one seems to know how the bonus scale is determined," said one respondent, an IT project analyst at a cable television company in the northeast. "I received a bonus because I was perceived to be hardworking. It seemed somewhat subjective," another respondent said.

The remarks suggest that the more people know, the more likely they are to think that the system is fair. "I believe it is fair to a point," said a respondent at a manufacturing company in the Great Lakes region. "The bonus amount changes the higher up you are, the theory being that the higher you are, the more influence you carry to help the corporation meet its goals."

Who gets what

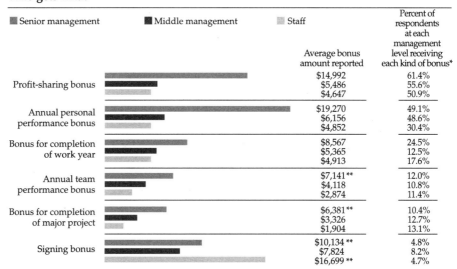

	Senior management	Middle management	Staff	Average bonus amount reported	Percent of respondents at each management level receiving each kind of bonus*
Profit-sharing bonus				$14,992	61.4%
				$5,486	55.6%
				$4,647	50.9%
Annual personal performance bonus				$19,270	49.1%
				$6,156	48.6%
				$4,852	30.4%
Bonus for completion of work year				$8,567	24.5%
				$5,365	12.5%
				$4,913	17.6%
Annual team performance bonus				$7,141**	12.0%
				$4,118	10.8%
				$2,874	11.4%
Bonus for completion of major project				$6,381**	10.4%
				$3,326	12.7%
				$1,904	13.1%
Signing bonus				$10,134**	4.8%
				$7,824	8.2%
				$16,699**	4.7%

Show me the money

The likelihood of your receiving a bonus depends on the type of bonus and the industry in which you work. These indexes show the chances of getting a particular type of bonus in various industries. The value 100 serves as the index average. This means, for example, that respondents in the transportation/utilities/communication carriers industry were 36 percent more likely than the average respondent to receive a profit-sharing bonus. Respondents in the business services sector were 42 percent less likely than average to receive signing bonuses.

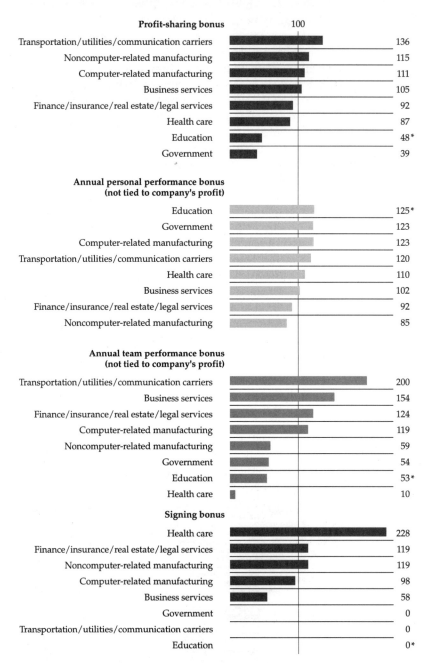

Profit-sharing bonus — 100

Industry	Index
Transportation/utilities/communication carriers	136
Noncomputer-related manufacturing	115
Computer-related manufacturing	111
Business services	105
Finance/insurance/real estate/legal services	92
Health care	87
Education	48*
Government	39

Annual personal performance bonus (not tied to company's profit)

Industry	Index
Education	125*
Government	123
Computer-related manufacturing	123
Transportation/utilities/communication carriers	120
Health care	110
Business services	102
Finance/insurance/real estate/legal services	92
Noncomputer-related manufacturing	85

Annual team performance bonus (not tied to company's profit)

Industry	Index
Transportation/utilities/communication carriers	200
Business services	154
Finance/insurance/real estate/legal services	124
Computer-related manufacturing	119
Noncomputer-related manufacturing	59
Government	54
Education	53*
Health care	10

Signing bonus

Industry	Index
Health care	228
Finance/insurance/real estate/legal services	119
Noncomputer-related manufacturing	119
Computer-related manufacturing	98
Business services	58
Government	0
Transportation/utilities/communication carriers	0
Education	0*

*Numbers marked with an asterisk are based on fewer than 30 respondents and are unstable.

WORK HOURS

There is lots to do and never enough time to do it. Although our survey results indicate that some IT professionals put in close to a standard workweek, many others work long hours and are on call far beyond forty hours.

The average work week reported by this year's respondents was 48.4 hours, about the same as in our 1998 survey. Senior managers go some way toward earning their high salaries with their average of 52.2 hours per week; middle managers reported working an average of 48.6 hours each week, and staff reported working 45.9 hours per week.

As the work hours chart shows, longer hours tend to be tied to higher salaries, probably at least in part because senior managers work the longest hours and earn the most money. A look at respondents' business or technology focus reveals a similar split. Focusing on both business and technology rather than solely on technology seems to result in more work to go along with the higher salaries, although this could be affected by the higher proportion of senior managers whose focus is split this way.

Some workers would dearly like to work fewer hours than they do, but many of them don't feel able to do that. A concern voiced by many respondents about cutting back on hours is the question of how the work would get done. "If I cut back, others would have to pick up the time, and it would not be fair to my peer employees," said a programmer analyst at an electric utility company in the midwest.

Others said they choose to put in more time in order to learn new skills and advance more quickly. "If I were willing to accept less advancement, I could [work less]," said an IT project manager at a large computer company in the northeast who reported no specific compensation or recognition for extra hours. "I know I've gotten promotions and raises for it, though," the project manager said. "Overall, I guess I do think it's adequate. That's why I'm not choosing fewer hours for less advancement."

Burning the midnight oil

Respondents reported working an average of 48.4 hours per week, but the people in some positions — especially senior management — put in more time. IT professionals in these five job categories tend to have the longest workweek.

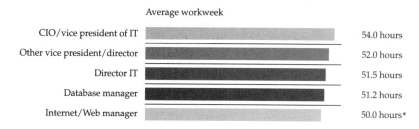

Average workweek

CIO/vice president of IT	54.0 hours
Other vice president/director	52.0 hours
Director IT	51.5 hours
Database manager	51.2 hours
Internet/Web manager	50.0 hours*

*Numbers marked with an asterisk are based on fewer than 30 respondents and are unstable.

Who ya gonna call?

For a majority of respondents at all levels, work extends beyond regular hours to being on call via pager or cell phone. However, very few receive compensation in return for their extra efforts.

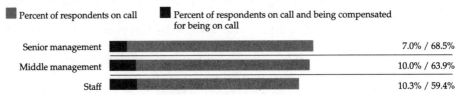

■ Percent of respondents on call	■ Percent of respondents on call and being compensated for being on call	
Senior management		7.0% / 68.5%
Middle management		10.0% / 63.9%
Staff		10.3% / 59.4%

A week in the life of IT

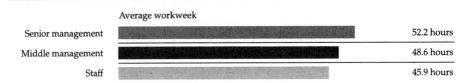

Average workweek

Senior management		52.2 hours
Middle management		48.6 hours
Staff		45.9 hours

EDUCATION

Advanced learning advances careers. To achieve that crucial balance between technical and business skills, IT professionals are turning to a variety of training and education methods.

Formal degrees remain the cornerstone; almost all of the survey respondents reported holding a degree of some sort. Of those, 16.4 percent said an associate's degree is their highest degree; 49.4 percent reported a bachelor's degree; and 30.5 percent reported a master's degree as their highest degree. Senior managers were more likely than middle managers or staff members to have advanced degrees, and at every level, salaries were higher for people with more education.

They're certified

A relatively small number, about one-fifth, of the respondents in the compensation survey answered this question. Among those, the MCSE certification is the most prevalent type.

Percent of respondents who reported holding certifications*

Microsoft Certified Systems Engineer	30.6%
Certified Novell Engineer	23.8%
Database certification	9.4%
Web certification	4.2%

*Numbers represent percentage of those who reported holding any certification. Multiple responses are possible.

Learning is a good thing

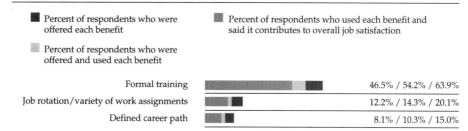

■ Percent of respondents who were offered each benefit

□ Percent of respondents who were offered and used each benefit

■ Percent of respondents who used each benefit and said it contributes to overall job satisfaction

Formal training	46.5% / 54.2% / 63.9%
Job rotation/variety of work assignments	12.2% / 14.3% / 20.1%
Defined career path	8.1% / 10.3% / 15.0%

The prevalence of MBAs in IT

How likely is it that your colleagues have MBAs? These indexes show the chances of an IT professional in each job category or industry having an MBA, compared with the overall average for the survey. The value 100 serves as the index average, which means that a director of IT, for example, is 91 percent more likely than the average respondent to have an MBA. Likewise, an IT professional in the government sector is 18 percent less likely to have one.

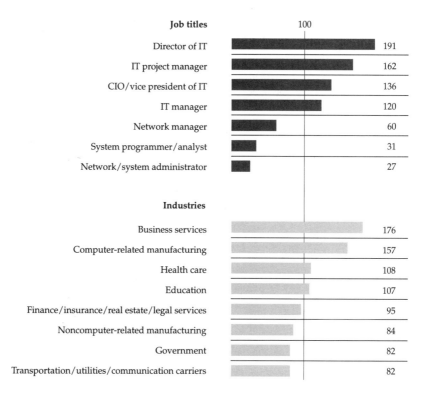

Job titles — 100

Director of IT	191
IT project manager	162
CIO/vice president of IT	136
IT manager	120
Network manager	60
System programmer/analyst	31
Network/system administrator	27

Industries

Business services	176
Computer-related manufacturing	157
Health care	108
Education	107
Finance/insurance/real estate/legal services	95
Noncomputer-related manufacturing	84
Government	82
Transportation/utilities/communication carriers	82

Business degrees were popular among respondents, particularly in certain job categories. One respondent reported that a technical bachelor's degree plus an MBA had provided a jump-start into project-lead roles. "[Education] has made it easier to work with engineers and corporate management," said another respondent, a software consultant with a bachelor's degree in engineering and an MBA.

One of the most contentious issues in the IT education arena is the value of certification. We asked our respondents which certifications they held and compared the salaries of those with certifications to those without. We found that at the staff level, people with Microsoft Certified Systems Engineer or Certified Novell Engineer certification earned more than staff members who did not have those certifications. At the middle management and senior management levels, there were no consistent patterns.

Does this mean that staff members should all get certifications unless they want to become managers? Probably not. More likely, it's a sign that certification may help boost a staff member's salary in some circumstances, and you need to carefully consider all the particulars of your situation before deciding.

METHODOLOGY

The statistical portion of the 1999 *InfoWorld* Compensation Survey was conducted by the IDG Research Services Group, an *InfoWorld* affiliate based in Framingham, MA.

In January, 7,000 confidential surveys were mailed; 137 were returned as undeliverable, bringing the total number of surveys delivered to 6,683. Of the 6,683 surveys delivered, 1,724 were completed, returned, and included in the results of the study, producing a 25 percent response rate. The sample for this study was selected on a random, "nth" name basis among *InfoWorld* subscribers with IT-related primary job functions. To ensure that the results of the study reflected the profile of *InfoWorld* subscribers who are IT professionals, the results were weighted to match the computer-related budget distribution for those subscribers.

APPENDIX C

Let's Continue the Conversation on the Web

The print version of *Internet Jobs!* is a powerful guide to the world of Net careers, but as a resource for online investigation, it really begins to add value. As comprehensive as *Internet Jobs!* is, no book can hold a candle to the limitless possibilities of a Web site as your window to finding Net jobs.

The *Internet Jobs!* Web site extends the book you are holding in your hands in a number of critical ways. A book has traditionally been an excellent resource for research, information, and knowledge, but then you had to take that research and information and make it actionable by sending a resume or making a phone call. The Web combines the elements of research and action. By creating interactivity, personalization, and community, Web sites enable researchers to act seamlessly on the information they research. On the Web, in the same breath you investigate a career possibility, you can fill out a questionnaire, send a resume, or fill out a resume template. It's all about interactivity and community. On the *Internet Jobs!* Web site, you will find abundant opportunities to continue your exploration of Net careers and to continue the conversation with the author that you started by buying this book.

So point your browser to *http://www.jkador.com/netjobs* for

- Highlights from *Internet Jobs!*
- Updates and links to the One Hundred Hottest Net Companies
- Updates and links to the Fifty Hottest Net Places to Live and Work
- Link to *The Contractors Handbook*

- The *Contractors Bill of Rights*
- Links to *InfoWorld* resources
- Links to other Net Economy salary surveys
- Links to other career sites
- Glossary of Net terms
- Conversation with the author and members of the *Internet Jobs!* community

About the Author

If you want to know more about my education, job history, freelance writing clients, and fee structure, you can find all that on my Web site (www.jkador.com).

Index